LEARNING TO SOAR

LEARNING TO SOAR

MEMOIR OF A SPIRITUAL AWAKENING

WIN BLEVINS

This book is dedicated to three extraordinary human beings—

Meredith, my beloved wife and partner in all ways,

The Honorable Clyde Hall, Shoshone, a judge of the tribal court, my great friend who taught me how to see with the single eye of the heart, how to carry the sacred pipe, and how to journey to another world,

And Joseph M. Marshall III, Brulé Lakota, the author of good books about all matters Lakota, and for me a helpful guide, wise counselor, and good friend.

TABLE OF CONTENTS

1. From Darkness into Light

This book is a story of taking a path from darkness toward spiritual light. The journey was tooth-and-nail hard. It has been spectacularly rewarding.

I came from the spiritual funk of a youth immersed in fundamentalist religion. After a crisis of faith, I walked a long trail over metaphorical mountains and sailed ghostly oceans before I could see clearly the grand carnival called life. This life is jam-packed with pratfalls, tears, cheers, anger, elation, grief, grace, and joy in simply being alive. Through the guidance of good, wise friends, and after being grounded for years, I got to s0ar high.

I am grateful. Happy. The longer I live, the more in living there is to love. I write as much as I can. Some days the writing is tough, and on some it's waggle-your-tail fun. I do art, which I enjoy thoroughly. And I try to return to playing the keyboard and singing to my own accompaniment. Music is ever with me. Sometimes I think we human beings, all of our atoms, vibrate with the music of the spheres, and we do it 24/7.

I love my wife Meredith every day. She makes it all good. I enjoy my children and grandchildren, though they live at a distance. My friends are treasures, and most are becoming more eccentric—

that's wonderful. Some of them have parted, but I still talk with them. (Hello, Gil. Hello, Rudy. Hi, Jeb.) I welcome each day as it comes. The sun is always rising.

Troubles in life? Stumbles? Sure. But as Vivian Greene said, "Life isn't about waiting for the storm to pass. It's about **learning to dance** in the **rain**." I've seen that on more than one refrigerator magnet. You never know where a bite out of wisdom's apple will appear.

In these pages I retrace the journey, starting in darkness and ending in what seems to me glory.

I invite you to join me. Perhaps an old man's trail markers can help you along the way. Stranger things, after all, have happened.

2. SETTING OUT

I wanted to soar into life, but I was scared.

At seventeen years of age, frozen by fear, I passed up a suggestion by Princeton University that I go to Princeton. (!) Instead, I took a safe, fearful step into the world. I chose to go to a two-year Bible college close to home. Safe, and as it turned out, very sorry.

That was the first of plenty of mistakes, most of them caused by the human being enemy number one, fear.

First step, which was a misstep: I found myself, one month into my second year at the junior college, sitting at the desk in my dormitory room in a pickle, or a rage, or the like.

As the editor of the school newspaper, I had put a picture of a ballerina in a ballet that was coming to town on page one. When the paper came out, the school burst into flames of anger. The professor of my next class and all his students spent the entire hour berating me. *Dance*—of all sins!—on page one, and in a revealing costume! *We don't believe in dance!*

I endured the hour and left the room near tears.

When I saw the ballet, though, I felt transported into a new and glorious world, a world where human beings move with a grace and beauty I hadn't imagined.

The next morning I woke up to find myself stuck in a dreary room for a week end alone, accompanied only by thoughts of how my classmates and the professor had denounced ballet, which I loved, as iniquitous. In the Southern Baptist tradition they rejected dance as sin: It was sensual, a fall into bodily temptation.

But I loved it.

This was a war on several fronts. At this college going to movies was frowned on unless the movie preached the Bible, as the movie *The Ten Commandments* had done. But I loved going to movies. As a kid I'd spent most Saturday afternoons at the matinees. Now I wanted to go to the local theater for whatever was on every Saturday night.

In music the college preference was hymns. I couldn't be bothered to learn that stiff-marching church music, but I liked to play Bach and Beethoven and thought I might like to play some pop music. I loved to watch Elvis Presley on television—look at those hips go! —and "Heartbreak Hotel" made me want to dance.

I sat in that dormitory room alone, on a campus of students who didn't accept me. I had one large thought: I don't belong here.

Though I didn't know it, I was about to jump off a cliff.

Stalling, I looked out the latticed window above my desk and across fields of grass beginning to turn to autumn colors. Beyond rolled the Mississippi, which I loved. It was a balm. A thought came to me: Mark Twain lived here and often fished and went swimming in that river. He finally became a steamboat pilot and rode the river from St. Louis all the way to New Orleans, a cauldron of sin. Later he went to San Francisco and dallied with low women. There he wrote and wrote and turned himself into a famous writer and ...

Whoops! Were my thoughts going astray?

Maybe I should write myself a letter. Maybe, sitting here, looking out at Mark Twain's river, I should tell myself what I think. Really think.

Fiercely, I wrote in block capitals at the top of the page:

WHAT I KNOW

Down the left-hand margin, I made a list:

Jehovah is creator of the world and everything in it.
He made it, and two human beings, male and female, in seven days.
Adam sinned, and thus are all men sinners.
I was born in original sin.
God is love.
And thus He gave His only begotten Son to save us all.
Jesus Christ is my personal savior.
Jesus died for my sins and so saved me.
He will save you.

Never the mind the rest—you know the sort of stuff.

I filled the cursed page, flipped it, and kept listing everything I'd learned as a child and youth, right down going to church twice on Sunday (with every prayer ending "In Jesus's name, amen") to the ritual of eating fried chicken for every Sunday dinner (introduced by a grace ending, naturally, in "In Jesus's name, amen.")

Then, slowly, thoughtfully, irresistibly, I crossed out every single line on those two pages.

All baloney, and I knew it. Knew it in my blood. My cells knew it. My tail on the chair knew it.

So, painfully, like amputating my arms and legs, I drew a big X over each side of that piece of paper.

Now I was an orphan. I had cut myself off from my parents, my rearing, my Baptist family and their Baptist forbearers, the world of mind and feeling I grew up in.

Was I sure?

Yeah, I was sure. I *knew*. I choked back the anger I felt at all the silly fantasies I'd been foolish enough to believe.

I wadded up the piece of paper and hurled it so hard into the bottom of the metal waste basket that it bounced out.

There goes my life, skittering across the floor.

The next morning I couldn't get up. What would I get up for? Not to go to church, no, no, not any more. I lay on the bed and stared at the ceiling, waiting in suspended disbelief, afraid to take a deep breath.

I laid there all day, inert, able to breathe but nothing more.

Saved by my roommate. Early in the evening my roommate Jim walked in from sinning with his girlfriend, or at least trying to. I blurted it straight out.

"Jim, I'm an atheist."

"Yeah," he said with a wry smile, "me too."

I'm not alone! Maybe I could survive eight more months of living among people who felt like aliens.

It turned out that there were four of us unbelievers in a college population of about three hundred—aside from me and Jim there were a son of Baptist missionaries to China and an older gay guy. The gay man was a lifeline to us other three, wiser in the ways of the world. He said the next college, *wherever* we went next year, would be different, and far better.

But I wanted more than *different*. I wanted liberation. I wanted to soar.

3. ON THE SEARCH

Ten years later: The secular worlds of university after university were challenging and exciting. Bachelor's and master's degrees came in order, and even marriage. The arrival of two great children brought a good feeling. I wasn't soaring yet, but a decade had passed since *that day*. Then I had a great stroke of luck: The Rockefeller Foundation offered to fund me through a two-year program to become a music critic.

Onward. After those years the two big Los Angeles newspapers gave me an opportunity as a music critic, then theater critic, then movie critic. *Great!*

I threw myself into these exciting challenges, and a lot about life was good.

And yet... And yet I was unhappy, dissatisfied.

Slowly I began to realize why: I still wasn't soaring. Instead of creating books and movies myself, I was spending my life commenting on what my friends in the worlds of movies and art were doing. They were writing books and scripts, they were performing behind the footlights or in front of the camera. And I? – In the pages of a newspaper I was *commenting* on what *they* were doing.

Clear enough: I had to admit that I was sitting on the bank of the river of life and watching—while my friends were in the water, splashing, horsing around, diving, swimming...

Yes, I was dissatisfied. My life wasn't enough. Sure, I got to go to lots of movies, plays, and concerts. Sure, I had lots of friends in those worlds. But my life felt flat and joyless.

When people mentioned spirituality, I could be disagreeable. I grimaced and turned away, scoffing internally. About those matters I had only negative thoughts. I disbelieved, disliked, dis- dis-, dis-, different styles of dissatisfaction. I was a Great White Doubter, and life does not sing *hallelujah* in the key of doubt. Skepticism is a barren land where nothing grows.

CHANGE: After two years of writing criticism (and who loves a critic?), I decided to take one step, a big step, toward my own rescue. I made myself a promise that I would quit my job as a damned critic and put myself on the other side. I would write my own books or movies. Let the critics write about what *I'm* doing.

I considered carefully. I had responsibilities. I needed to support myself and two kids from a failed marriage. I needed to get real in taking this step. *Can I make a living?*

So I gave myself two more years to find a way, somehow. To back that up, I set myself a deadline—summer of 1972. A real deadline—I would damn well meet it, though I had no idea how.

Maybe it was time for the Great White Doubter to surrender doubt and ask the universe to give me a blessing. But didn't that approach sound almost … spiritual?

Get thee behind me, dirty word. And look out, world, here I come.

4. WILL THE
UNIVERSE SMILE ON ME?

The crucial year of 1972 came with no hope in sight.

Then I thought I saw a glimmer: Al Ruddy, producer of *The Godfather,* wanted to make a thousand-page novel (never mind the title) into a movie. For some reason he came to me and asked me to write what the film industry calls a bible for it—my first movie job.

It was a daunting task. Such a long book. I had to cut enough characters and scenes to squeeze it into a three-hour picture, which meant a draft of about one hundred and eighty pages.

OK. I thought I knew what to cut and what to shorten. I took the assignment. It was my first footing in the film business.

In the industry a bible is a full account of every scene that will be in the picture, with all characters on hand, the action described, and the dialogue summarized. It is a detailed outline for a motion picture.

After working days at the newspaper, I put in long nights at the typewriter and did the work for Ruddy in a couple of weeks. I re-read the manuscript and felt proud of it.

Then Ruddy's secretary called. Never mind the bible—the production was cancelled.

Naturally, Ruddy didn't pay me for the work. He was a producer.

Maybe universe wasn't smiling on me—it was laughing at me.

And then, abruptly, everything changed. The universe became a beaming mistress.

This report of striving to become a professional writer—is it a detour away from the subject of my spiritual life? No. At least for me, spiritual awareness has come through opening the door to creativity, discovering the benevolence of the universe, and being grateful.

Just a few weeks later, at a party at a fine house high In Beverly Hills, I was talking to a good friend, Dale Wasserman, the author of *Man of La Mancha*. We were having fun trading stories about the mountain men, the guys who went to the Rocky Mountains ahead of everyone else, found ways to get along with the Indians, learned the territory, and risked their lives to make money trapping the wily beaver.

I paid no attention to the fellow who sat in the next chair, listening to our stories. But before the evening ended, he sought me out.

"I'm Ed Nash."

Seeing that I didn't understand, he added, "owner of Nash Publishing."

Wow. The only significant book publisher in Los Angeles. Now he had my full attention.

"Would you have lunch with me tomorrow?" he asked. "Talk about writing a book for Nash?"

WRITE A BOOK? WOULD I?

I stammered, "Yes."

At lunch he asked me if I had an idea for a book. I gave him a terrible idea. He asked, instead, if I would tell the stories Dale and I had told last night at the party, about the mountain men.

Could I write those? Would I? After all, as he pointed out, the mountain men were almost unknown.

Inside I was screaming, *Could I? Would I?* A merry-go-round was circling madly in my heart, playing circus music. I'd first heard those stories from my great teacher John G. Neihardt at the University of Missouri. He made them enchanting. I could make them enchanting again.

My inner calliope was celebrating loudly, but I didn't let Ed Nash hear.

I said, "Sure."

"How big of an advance would you want?"

I calculated quickly. How long would I need to write the book? Maybe a year? What would I earn in salary at the newspaper in a year?

"7500.00," I said.

He said, "I think we can do better than that," and offered ten thousand dollars. Stunned, I squeezed out a yes.

Done deal.

Lesson to self and all writers: Don't negotiate for yourself. You're lousy at it. And when you have an offer on the table, it's *easy* to get an agent. Ed Nash would probably have given twice what I asked for. (And later the book earned it.)

There was also something bigger to think about. I had pledged to work as a critic until the middle of 1972 and then risk all and *quit my job.*

Now I had a deal that paid me to write a book—paid me a full year's salary. Self and two kids now supported.

Was the universe a better place than I'd thought? Maybe it was time to retire the Great White Doubter.

Could I do that? Was I ready to let go of a quarter century of energetic skepticism?

I tucked that thought away for future consideration.

5. $\mathscr{A}$ NEW WORLD

I felt strongly that Ed Nash's overhearing me tell some stories and offering me a book contract was the great piece of luck I'd been hoping for—enough, in fact, for me to quit playing The White Doubter.

After a short distance down that road I was as lost as I could be.

Nash Publishing soon spoiled my debut as a writer of books. After selling nearly ten thousand copies in a rush, the company was unable to reprint the book, thousands of orders went unfilled, and I made very little money on royalties.

Before I discovered how miserably Nash was treating me, I signed a contract to write another book, wrote it, and turned it in. Nash accepted it and published it. Two days after publication the company went out of business. Talk about a quick way to kill a book. And to revive the Great White Doubter.

Now 1975, three years after meeting Ed Nash by accident, I was lost. My job was gone for good. The book road was looking very, very rocky. Who said this was a friendly universe?

But I had a feeling about something I wanted to write, a marvelous story I wanted to tell. I'd read a *tall* stack of books about the West—not that cowboy stuff, the larger West, the West that had mythic size and yet was *real*. And I'd fallen in love with a Sioux warrior and chieftain named Tashunke Witko, or His Horses Dance in a Sacred Way, generally known as Crazy Horse. Though his story had been told by several writers, I sensed some meaning in his life that was larger and more marvelous. I yearned to find it and show it in my pages.

And at the same time it scared the hell out of me.

Crazy Horse raised my demons. He governed his life by visions.

Whoops! Visions were one of the great bugaboos of my life. In my mind believing in visions was listening to burning bushes that talk. It was the way of crackpots who disappeared into the desert to starve and pray for some mad truth. I could no more admire a man of visions than I could be a snake handler.

Yet something within me *loved* something about Crazy Horse. Out of the darkness he was calling to me—*come, see, understand, feel.*

I got in my car and headed out of Los Angeles to spend a summer driving all over the West looking for Crazy Horse. I would go where he'd gone, stand where he stood, wade the creeks he waded, pull his air deep into my lungs.

My writing world was the historical West and how it shaped the nation we came to be. I read another tall stack of books, looking for the story I wanted to tell. I was entranced by the thought that I had to find the elusive, entrancing Sioux warrior and chieftain named Crazy Horse. I had to find in him a way that wasn't recognized. He was something more, I sensed, something I wanted to understand. I would go to the reservations where the Sioux (Lakota) people lived and seek out their stories about him, explore their memories. I would find something elusive, something that drew me, something that would haunt me until I found it.

That summer I roamed through Lakota country and talked to Lakota people and did my best to conjure up a man dead for a hundred years.

I came back with a conviction: I had to tell his story.

And with a great fear of the obstacles that stood in my way: I had to make peace, somehow, with the importance of visions to this man. Because if he was literally Crazy, I wouldn't be able to write about him. I had to overcome great obstacles: I didn't speak his language, know his customs, understand his ways, and get past thinking he was crazy.

Bottom line: I needed to step into his mind, turn around, look out at the world through his eyes, and *see* it.

I *had* to tell his story. And that meant I had to do the work, do the work, do the work, until I was able to see, sense, feel this world as he did.

Steps forward: I moved with my new wife to Wyoming, walked the earth where he walked it, drank the water, breathed the air. And I asked Lakota people, and others of the Native world, to show me how they understand this life, until I began to see.

(A practical matter: During this time I wrote two other novels to pay the rent, buy the groceries, in general ease the way.)

I got two amazing blessings that lit the path. You're entitled to think they were terrific strokes of luck or gifts of a benevolent universe or whatever you like. They enriched my life enormously.

The first was that I met Clyde Hall, a man from the nearby Shoshone reservation. Though Clyde was a Shoshone, he had gone to live with the Lakota medicine man Leonard Crow Dog at his place, Crow Dog Paradise, for a year and a half and there had learned Lakota ways like how to pour a sweat lodge and how to go on a vision quest.

Right away Clyde took me into a sweat lodge. I got an inkling of spiritual power in the lodge, and went back. Soon Clyde began to talk to me about visions. I *listened.* This was I'd come for.

And with amazing swiftness I got it.

I told Clyde how skeptical I was. He probed. And before long he ferreted this story of me. It was literally true and absolutely stunning:

6. $\mathcal{I}$ GO SOARING

FOR THE FIRST TIME

A psychotherapist friend let me know that he had an empty slot in a session he'd set up. Sometimes that happened, and he would invite me to watch and listen. He knew I learned as a writer by listening to people in group therapy. But no one was to know I wasn't a participant, just like everyone else.

As it happened, the one empty seat in his living room was next to Judy, a friend from the Hearst newspaper where we both worked. She got the first chance to talk during the session, and what she said amazed me. As a teenager she'd been a heroin addict and a prostitute. She escaped from both lives eight years ago, but wanted to know …

She wasn't sure what.

I was stunned. In the six or seven years I'd known her, Judy had done nothing but command my respect. (And now she had even more respect.)

My friend the psychotherapist—for discretion let's call him Psycho—decided to hypnotize her, which I'd seen him do a number of times, and had experienced myself. He wanted to do age regression with her. This I hadn't seen, and I was doubtful that such a thing was possible.

Psycho took Anne back to the age of five, and got her to describe in amazing detail exactly where she was and what was going on, a fight with her mother. At some point she said, "That's when I knew—my parents were crazy."

OK, I ask you to believe what I'm about to describe very literally. This is exactly what happened:

My body went off like a rocket from a launching pad, blew through the ceiling, through the roof, through the atmosphere, and into outer space.

It was very, very lonely out there, and very black. I recognized absolutely nothing, not a planet, not a moon, not a star, nothing. I knew I must be an incredibly long way from the solar system that was my home.

Looking around, I saw a flagstone path leading... Where? Anywhere. Everywhere.

I got down on my knees and brushed the sandstone with my fingertips. I looked down its path. This was exhilarating—I felt a wild desire to follow it, to explore it to wherever it might go, to the far reaches of...

Who knew? The adventure was *not* knowing.

As I stood up, I saw some friends, no more than ten, but good friends.

How great! They were here to go with me! We'd explore together.

Happiness galloped in me like the bulls through Pamplona.

So I started out, leading the way along the flagstones. It was an easy path.

For a while.

Before long the stones began to get further apart, so that I had to stretch or even hop from one to the next. But who cared? This was fun. This was adventure.

16

I glanced back and noticed that a couple of friends were hesitating, then dropping out. Who cared? Excitement led me forward.

Soon the path changed again. The stones began to tilt, making the footing uncertain. And now I saw that I'd lost several more friends.

I looked into the vast unknown.

I was ecstatic, having the time of my life.

The flagstones got further apart, and now I had to leap from one to the next. I lost a couple of more friends.

The leaps got longer, and the angles of the stones got steeper. I really had to watch my footing. But I felt sure I wouldn't fall, shrieking, into the sheer emptiness and blackness of space. I grinned at my buddies. I saw that I was down to just three of them.

Strange. How could anyone resist? This adventure was going somewhere no one had ever been. It was the ultimate adventure.

Hey, didn't Richard Dreyfuss walk onto that space ship at the end of *Close Encounters of the third Kind*? Did anyone doubt that he would? Wouldn't *everyone* do the same? Go for the bounding elation of adventure?

I would. I did.

Leap, find my footing, regain balance.

Harder yet.

Do it again.

And then again.

Until I came to a place that was impossible.

Looked impossible.

Far too much empty space—and we're talking *space* here—to jump across. No chance.

I looked and looked.

Hey, maybe something. *There*, right there, was a nexus of energy—nothing solid, just a whirl of energy spinning around itself in one small spot.

I turned and looked back and only one companion was still with me. Joanne, my best friend from years before, and whom I'd later had a wild affair with.

All right. She's the one I want most anyway.

I turned and looked back at that ball of energy. Then I understood. It was an exercise in mathematics. I had to run equations in my head until I solved the problem, exactly how to make a quick, light step onto that energy, get just enough of a push to leap on to...

I was not great at equations, but by God I would do it.

I turned and looked back at Joanne. Her face was fixed, regal, and wet with tears.

I looked and looked at her and at last understood.

I would be able to go on, but the woman I had loved most would not. None of my friends would.

Joanne was grieving. Her eyes were saying goodbye. Goodbye forever.

I knew. I knew-knew.

At the same time I also knew I would go on.

I was born to this, to *go!*

I turned and looked into an infinite vista of vistas.

Music thrummed throughout my body, it was my blood, it was the heartbeat of sadness.

I looked at that nexus of energy. My mind flashed with numbers. I saw an answer. I could see my destiny. It was absolutely clear.

I raised my foot for the crucial step, raised my eyes and my heart to the adventure, and stepped into the unknown...

7. In the "Real" World

Back in that Beverly Hills living room I was bawling.

Yes, bawling, uncontrollably.

Psycho gently asked me to be quiet, and I stifled the tears.

He and Judy kept talking about her experience as though nothing had happened, and for them it hadn't.

I said nothing about what I'd seen. Not then, not later. Oddly, my friend Psycho never asked me. No one did. And I sure didn't want to talk about it.

It had been one of the most vivid mental experiences I'd ever had, waking or dreaming. And it didn't feel like either one. It felt like watching a movie. I was intensely part of the movie and at the same time aware of my surroundings, hearing the voices of Judy and Psycho (without taking in the meaning of their words). It didn't feel at all like a dream. I was wholly in the midst of the movie's action. I had no way to understand it, yet felt I felt that my mind, or some wise part of me, was trying to tell me something hugely important.

I replayed it in my head every day. But I was too much embarrassed to speak of it to anyone.

Certainly I hadn't had a vision. Visions didn't exist.

So I needed an explanation that wasn't super-natural. Had I hitchhiked along on Psycho's hypnotic induction of Judy? Hmmm. I hadn't gone where he led her.

I had no idea what happened. And I wasn't going to open my mouth and make a fool of myself.

For some reason, though I had the issue of Crazy Horse's visions right in front of me, I didn't think of my flight through the skies as a hint. Why? Childhood. My forebears had believed in ghosts (ha'nts), in those who spoke in tongues, handled rattlesnakes, and hoped bushes would spontaneously start burning and speak truth. The last thing I wanted was to go back to being one of them.

The last.

I refused to have a dialogue with myself about it. I was still holding hard to the idea that from Moses and the burning bush to Joseph Smith and the angel—all mystic revelations were either a touch of madness or just plain hokum.

Too bad. The world (or some mysterious something) had sent me a signal as high, wide, loud, and destructive-creative as a lightning storm, and I hadn't caught on.

So I didn't get any help from this super-dramatic experience of soaring. Yet.

I set in to doing what writers do—write. I had a contract, a good one with a major publisher, and by God I would do the book.

Handling visions? I would let that come to me.

This is a quirky behavior, maybe, that fiction writers use. (We're all half crazy.) We think of the kernel of a story, maybe just a sudden dilemma that faces a character, and we jump in without knowing anything more, confident that ideas will come when called for (or faking ourselves into confidence).

So I jumped in and wrote Crazy Horse's story as energetically as I could, taking time off only to go climb mountains and stand in the unemployment line.

It didn't work. About fifty pages in (the effort of two or three months) I took the pages to lunch one day, read them, and knew—it wasn't working. Flat out wasn't working. A writer gets that dead-sure feeling. I set the book of my heart aside and set sail on another story.

Onward. I wrote several books and scripts in this on-again-off-again way. I would write a novel (in maybe a year) and get it started with the publisher. Then rev up again on Crazy Horse and charge forward for two or three months, and know it wasn't working. Then write a script (a couple of months) and give it to some producer (temporary relief from the unemployment lines). Then put the quirt to myself and ride forward with Crazy Horse, and realize it wasn't working.

Two years into the journey the publisher, Houghton Mifflin, got impatient and opted out.

Stumped, I decided to persist, and that's what I did. Did it for a dozen more years before getting a breakthrough. Sometimes I made excuses other than my inability to understand Our Strange Man fully. It might be impossible to lead a wide audience to see the story of the West—which Americans regarded as a heroic triumph—from the point of view of the Indian people whose way of life was destroyed by it. Yet I wanted to create just that understanding. I told myself, and believed, and still believe, that if we can't understand each other, there's damn little hope for the human race.

I didn't intend to be stopped.

After five years I pulled up stakes in Malibu and moved to Wyoming. Partly I wanted to get away from Los Angeles and give my heart to the mountains. Mostly I wanted mostly to gallop the prairies Crazy Horse galloped, ford the rivers he forded, chase the antelope he chased, smell the air he smelled, feel the cold winds of winter he endured, and feel the same summer sun on my skin. I wanted to inhabit his skin and look out through his eyes.

My fascination with Our Strange Man scared me, but held me.

A couple of years into that difficult period, a mutual friend suggested that I call Clyde Hall, a man living on the Shoshone reservation about an hour from my home in Jackson Hole. I got him on the phone, asked him to lunch, and had fine time. A good man, very good, and smart. He was a tribal judge there on the rez.

Over the next couple of years our friendship got special. I was still passionate about learning to understand the Lakota, and Clyde, by the happiest of fates, was Lakota in his ceremonial practices. Therein lies a story, and a boon for me.

The Honorable Clyde Hall, Judge, Shoshone Tribe, my dear friend and mentor

In 1973, when the armed occupation of Wounded Knee ended, Clyde headed for Crow Dog Paradise, the home of the principal medicine man of the occupiers of Wounded Knee, Leonard Crow Dog. Clyde stayed for six months, devoting himself to learning all he could about the Lakota way from Leonard and his grandfather, Henry Crow Dog, both renowned medicine men. Then Clyde spent a year living with a very traditional Lakota family and learning more about the traditional ways.

Because of that training, Clyde's sweat lodges were conducted in the Crow Dog family way, which is not the Shoshone way and is different even from some Lakota practice. He sings some songs in the Lakota language, and conducts a number of ceremonies in the way the Crow Dogs taught him. His ceremonial path is a blend of Lakota and Shoshone.

Luckily, Clyde did not and does not want most of these practices kept secret—quite the opposite. He believes strongly in a kind of missionary work to the white people of America. "The way of the pipe is for everyone," he told me over and over. "In fact, it may be what keeps this crazy world from destroying itself."

From my point of view, the student was ready and the teacher had appeared.

So this man became my mentor. We did sweats together, I learned how to build a sweat, and eventually he taught me how to be the sweat leader, pouring the water on the super-heated lava rocks to make the steam explode upward, saying the traditional prayers, and singing songs in Shoshone, Lakota, and (he added) in English or any other language Spirit suggested. I have done all of those things.

Somehow praying was all right with me now. I was a little uneasy with the word itself. I preferred to say "calling to." But I trusted Clyde. He asked me to bow down to no god, and he called to the Sky, Earth, the Four Winds and other "Powers." This seems to me different. These powers are genuine forces in our lives on this planet.

Before long I came to a great realization. To Clyde, and perhaps most wise Indian people, "Spirit" means the force that vivifies everything—the turn of the Earth around the sun, the rising of the sap in the trees, the fecundity of Mother Earth, the strength of Moon that moves the oceans themselves, the power of the Wind to bring thunderstorms, the amazing gifts of light and heat from Father Sun. and much, much more—everything.

After several years I took the big step, not because I wanted to learn more about Crazy Horse, though I did, but because I was aware that these sweats, and the dances I went to, were good for my spirits. If I went in feeling troubled, I came out feeling brimming with energy.

So I told Clyde I wanted to become a carrier of the sacred pipe (as I still am).

He welcomed me to the red road. I wanted to make a simple pipe, as of an unimportant man, because that's what Crazy Horse did. We sought and found a fallen limb from the right tree and of the right size and peeled off the bark to reveal a beautiful piece of wood, with a natural red stripe down the middle. The stripe felt like a blessing.

I carved the piece of wood to the necessary shape. I ordered a bowl from the well-known quarry in Minnesota, red Catlinite with a Four Winds design. A cousin of Clyde's beaded a fine bag for my pipe.

Then, much more important, Clyde conducted a dedication ceremony for me as a pipe carrier, based on the ceremony handed down from the Lakota George Sword. I was carefully instructed in ceremonial handling of the pipe.

Cedar is used to cleanse the pipe and drive away bad influences. The bowl, which represents the earth, may be handled only with the left hand. The right hand, which represent all growing things, holds the stem toward the body.

The pipe is consecrated in a sweat lodge (*inipi*) in a ceremonial way. It is lit and smoked by the man conducting the ceremony, and then in turn by the friends and witnesses gathered there. I was glad that my son Adam was one of these. Each man takes a few puffs of the sacred smoke, which is the breath of the *wakan* (holy), and says or thinks a short prayer mentioning the Powers being asked to give this pipe strength—each of the four directions, then Father Sky, Mother Earth, the seventh grandfather, who is the center of all things, and perhaps Sun, Moon, Stone, Thunderbird, or whatever seems right at the moment.

Normally, a pipe will go around the circle once, but not a full second time. The bowl of my pipe is smaller than a man's little finger. This pipe went around once, and around again. People began to smile—this was acting like a *wakan* (mysterious or sacred) pipe. When it was still burning after two circuits, Clyde joked about it being a never-ending pipe. Around it went a third time, and a fourth, to many chuckles, until finally all the tobacco was burned. Then Clyde emptied the ashes into the fire, so that they could not be stepped on or spat on or otherwise sullied.

Clyde enjoined the witnesses to keep an eye on me and if I ever misused the pipe, take it away and return it to Clyde. I revere the pipe, I smoke it, and I am honored to carry it.

The night of my pipe dedication the tribe was holding a dance, and we attended. Clyde asked me to dance along with him and told me to carry my pipe, now a vessel of power, in its bag.

I danced without my feet touching the earth.

Me a pipe carrier? Through a Lakota pipe ceremony supervised by a Shoshone?

A miracle.

My ceremonial materials for the sweat lodge—my pipe (which is divided into bowl and stem, as it must be when not being smoked), beaded pipe bag, an eagle wing, which is used to blow cleansing smoke around the lodge, and my eagle bone whistle, which is used to call the spirits to the lodge.

Not only is Clyde as much Lakota in ceremonial practice as Shoshone (I'm avoiding the word "religion," as he generally does), but also things change. Tribes see each other's ceremonies, borrow certain practices from each other, and learn certain songs from each other.

As I write now, we have a distinctively pan-Indian culture. For instance, I have been instructed scrupulously in how to build a sweat lodge in the Lakota way (actually the Crow Dog family's way), how to dig the hole for the fire shallow as a salad bowl, and how to sing a certain song in Shoshone to the red-hot lava rocks when we have brought them in, a song thanking the rocks for opening themselves (as though giving birth) to give us the heat and moisture.

At another time I was taught by Crow elders exactly how to build a lodge in their way (significantly different), how and where to dig the hole for rocks (their hole is like a pickle barrel), and so on. And in both cases I was encouraged to introduce songs of different languages, including English, if I felt so moved, and to sing any song that came to me spontaneously, if any did.

And, a little comically, I have been verbally corrected in performing the ceremony exactly in the Lakota way by a ... *Navajo*. The way he wanted is what I call pan-Indian, a mélange of traditions that now has general acceptance.

Clyde says things have always changed, and that is only right—when the change comes from what the leader of the ceremony feels led by Spirit to do, and if it is not a matter of carelessness or forgetfulness. Change is part of the tradition.

Though it has been years since I've seen Clyde—much to my regret—I still cherish my pipe. I smoke it in a spirit of gratitude. After making the traditional addresses to the four directions, Father Sky, and Mother Earth, I speak abundantly of my gratitude for everything life and this wonderful planet give us. I include what you might imagine and add gravity, for holding me to the earth, the air, for giving me oxygen, the song birds, for bringing music to my ears, and much, much, much-much more. I am full of joy at being alive.

That is the great gift years of spiritual seeking has brought me. I invite you to join in.

Now there is still a big story to tell.

8. HEADING FOR THE MOUNTAIN

After I became a pipe carrier, I wanted urgently to get the clarity to finish the book about Crazy Horse.

The first step was clear. As an act of faith, I had to go on the mountain, as seeking a vision is called—I had to learn to *see*.

As a first step, I told Clyde the unrecognized and unappreciated vision that had been given to me fifteen years earlier in front of Psycho. I had to push aside Win the Scaredy Cat and speak up.

Clyde and I did a sweat. After he got the lodge full of steam, invited the spirits to join us, and sang an introductory song, I told him, fumbling for words, what I had seen in my mental escapade long ago, from the rocket blast into outer space to following the stone path into infinity, to my last look back at the woman I loved and the thrill of going forward into the adventure alone.

There. I had done it. Now I didn't know who I was or what to think of myself.

Clyde's sweats usually go four rounds, and after my short tale he took the first break. When he started making steam again, Clyde teased me. "You say you don't believe in visions."

"Yeah."

"Yet you just told me the wildest lollapalooza of a vision I have ever heard."

A long silence while I held his words on my palate. "So that was a vision?"

He started to say "duh," but changed it to "yes."

"What did it mean?"

"You have some learning to do." And he threw open the lodge door for another break.

Back into the lodge, the darkness, the steam: The learning went like this: Visions are mysterious. Don't waste time asking how they happen, where they come from, and such as that. More important, no one knows the meaning of a vision but the one who has it. Because nothing could be more personal.

He looked at me through the whirling steam. "Ask your questions."

"Is it usual for what we see over there to seem more vivid, and more real, than the ordinary world? Like a technicolor movie?"

"It is reality," said Clyde. "The daily world is a kind of illusion, or a shadow of that true world."

I took a deep breath before asking the next question. "What is a vision, really? Is it a ... deity speaking to us?" I have trouble saying the G word.

He said nothing.

"Or someone or something in the Jungian collective unconscious calling out to us?"

Still nothing.

"Or part of our own subconscious telling us something because we haven't paid enough attention and need to be school-marmed?"

Silence again. He outwaited me. He just poured the water and in the mushrooming steam began to pray in a language I didn't know, probably Shoshone, and he sang songs in that language. I assumed he was asking the Powers to help me see, not the word-filled, analytical kind of seeing, but a true seeing with my whole self, every cell of me—seeing with the single eye of my heart.

During the short break between the second and third rounds, he said, "I don't know what part of the mind gives birth to visions, or opens the window to them, or ... It could be any of the parts you named, or maybe none. I don't know. I do know this. It is looking with the single eye of the heart, not the two eyes of the head."

I breathed that in, let it out. It fit. See life whole, instead of seeing part after part and trying to fit them together in your mind. Not seeing analytically but seeing all at once, with mind, senses, emotions, imagination, body, the whole being. I could accept this without understanding it, or experiencing it completely. "Seeing in a holistic way," I said. Maybe what D. H. Lawrence had called the knowledge of the blood. People in the South say, "I know it in my bones."

Clyde made an m-m-m-m sound that may have been assent, but was more likely, 'Some things are best not talked about.'

When I hear great music, I thought, *I don't think about it. I let it sweep through me. Nothing else exists at those moments, no thoughts, no images. It is like flying within the music. And afterwards there is nothing to think about, just a feeling having been ... transported to another world. Something like a vision.*

The last question, worth sixty-four thousand dollars: "What does it mean, what I saw?"

Clyde gave a tiny snort. "No one knows." Silence. "Over time you may have some thoughts about that. But remember, they are just that, thoughts *about* it. They are not the experience itself. Be careful always to preserve what you saw, and not cling to any conclusions about it. Then your understanding will grow beyond those conclusions, in a form that is real but wordless."

He was silent. "I suggest you hold it to your chest and feel it breathing like a child, heart to heart with you, or a stone heated in a fire to keep you warm.

"Still, you may decide it offers you certain lessons. Fine, just don't get stuck on them. Let them come as they will and change as they will. Don't analyze what you saw. Remember it, see it again and again. Whatever is there for you will seep into your entire self.

"That's enough for now."

Clyde spent the fourth round praying for me, that I might keep my feet on the red path, live in the power of my pipe, and see with the single eye of my heart.

After the last round, when we were relaxing outside, I asked. "Can a person call up such visions on purpose, persuade them to come to him at a certain time and place?"

After a hesitation Clyde said, "An experienced man can. One day we will talk about how."

I waited. Finally, I said, "I think that's enough questions for now."

Then we went to dinner. It's customary to give the man you are asking to give you good medicine a feast afterwards. These days that usually means a trip to a nearby restaurant, and on the Fort Hall rez there is only one.

As we walked to the car, I said, "There's more, isn't there?"

"There's always more," Clyde said.

"What's next?"

He said, "Decide whether you want to go on the mountain."

Cry for a vision.

I leapt off a cliff emotionally. "I'm gangbusters to go."

He was quiet while he thought. "Good. Bring me some gifts"—he named the traditional four, tobacco, a piece of red cloth a blanket, and a feast—"and ask to be put on the mountain. Then we do a sweat lodge and I tell you how my people traditionally do vision quests. The Shoshone way would mean twenty-four hours somewhere solitary, no food or water, lots of crying for a vision, and lots of awareness of what you see or don't see. Then another sweat for me to ... debrief you.

"The Lakota way would be similar with one big difference: Instead of one day without food or water, there are five. So which style, Shoshone or Lakota?"

"Shoshone the first time." I was scared of all that fasting, but sooner or later I would follow the path of Crazy Horse—five days.

"Bring the gifts."

He threw the door open to let the light in and the steam out.

I had expected to feel shaky. How could a man who knew for absolutely-positively sure that there were no such things as visions, how could this fellow admit that he personally had gone soaring on one?

Part of me had the weird feeling like I didn't know who I was any more, and needed to introduce me to myself. Most of me felt bounding with happiness.

A week later I brought the gifts, we built the sweat, and went in. He started with the traditional prayers. He told me what to do during my twenty-four hours, and instructed to come back for another sweat afterwards and tell him what I had seen or not seen. I was sure I would see nothing.

9. THE SEEKER GOES TO THE MOUNTAIN

The American English expression for it is "vision quest." The Lakotas say it is seeing beyond the apparent world to the real world.

Me, on a vision quest. Amazing. The man who came to scoff, and spent three decades doing that, was now staying to pray.

I'd chosen the Snake River Hot Springs for my first quest. Those springs are on the southeast edge of Yellowstone, and known mostly to locals. By car you drive north from Jackson through some of the world's most spectacular scenery, the straight north-south line of the Teton Mountains, thirteen thousand feet high and spectacularly jagged, perhaps the world's most photographed peaks. The Snake River flows past their feet, then a plain on the east side of the mountains and on the other side the Gros Ventre Mountains, creating the "hole" of Jackson Hole.

At this time of year, early autumn, all those mountains are a showcase of aspen leaves turning gold, or in many places bright flame. October, the month of my fifty-second birthday.

At the boundary between the national park and the national forest is a ranger station guarding the south entrance to Yellowstone. I go in and ask for a permit for the camping spot at the hot springs. Of course, it's available during this off-season. The families are gone, the kids back in school, and the park is easing from buzzing-bee crowds into its winter rest.

Also, the grizzlies are active at this time, grabbing everything they can get to eat before their long naps, and not as shy of people as usual. I have to sign a notice that I've been informed that the area is considered high-hazard grizzly territory right now. Fortunately, since I'll be fasting, I'm not carrying any food into the park to tempt them. *Except myself,* I think with a smile.

Get outside, shoulder the pack, and start walking. It's one of the great feelings, going for any long walk into unknown country, but especially along a gorgeous alpine river and into the wilds of so a grand park as Yellowstone. The hopes and fears I'm carrying intensify my sense of adventure.

First off, I ford the river. The water and the trail intertwine for some miles, but the next ford comes just beyond my camping spot.

In fording the river thigh-deep, somehow, I feel a change in the mode of awareness of my day-to-day brain, a crossing of an invisible boundary from the ordinary world of consciousness into a special space, a place where extraordinary things may happen, may be felt, be heard or seen. For the time of walking the next six miles, then twenty-four hours dedicated to crying for a vision, and the time to walk back, I will be silent except for prayer and song. I will be opening my eyes, ears, and mind—not just the eyes, ears, and mind that keep me informed about the everyday world, but the ones of my spirit.

I am a blank slate. I have no idea what may happen, or not happen. Never in my life have I walked into any territory where I had less idea where I was going. Even the physical destination, the hot springs, I have not seen before. And what about world beyond, as it's traditionally called? I have no idea. But I do have a box of tools. Clyde laid out some rituals for me to perform, words to utter and to others sing, attitudes that may show me a path, but where it leads…?

Right now I seek reassurance by telling myself that nothing will happen—I will cry for a vision but get none. Often that happens, I suspect, especially to neophytes. The new world, the one I hope I'm earning, will pay no attention to my desires.

I arrive at the springs, which are smoking. They're too hot to sit in except right where they mix with the river, which is melted snow. I would like the comfort of the waters but won't go into them on this visit. At this time, this place is not a spa.

I set down my pack, separate my secular and sacred belongings, and begin. I sit on a hillock and smoke my pipe, offering the smoke to the four directions—east, the home of the sun, the father all things, the south, the place of growth, the west, home of the thunderbirds and therefore of thunder and lightning, and the north, home of the White Giant. Last, I offer the smoke to Father Sky, Mother Earth, and (in a practice that is the choice of some seekers) the seventh grandfather, the center of myself, which is synchronous with the center of the universe.

The smoke of this *cansasa*, tobacco, when coming from a dedicated *canupa*, pipe, is the breath of these *wakan Tunkashila*, Grandfathers, whose power I ask to come to me. This first prayer is a declaration that I seek a vision and ask for their help in learning to see.

Then I sit and watch the wildlife. Here along the river I see mostly birds, many ravens and a couple of bald eagles. Any animal can be the bearer of a vision, or part of one, or come as a spirit animal, but eagles especially are likely to be *wakan* (sacred) and messengers of the Powers. I see the birds but hear no messages, and sense none.

After a few minutes I find some sticks, shove two crossed pairs into the ground about a foot apart, lay another stick horizontally across their forks, and prop my pipe against it. A basic altar for my time here.

Now I walk in a wide circle around the camp. It is in a big meadow of straw-colored grasses, and in some places red grasses.

Along the border of grasses and pine trees I see grizzly scat here and there. I see no message in that, and no threat.

I go back to my pipe, smoke it, and then sing one of the songs I learned in the sweat lodge. Then I simply sit, watch, and listen, keeping my mind blank. Nothing yet.

When the sun is just a few minutes above the mountains in the west—they are very high, so we will have a long twilight—I gather about two dozen calf-high twigs to make a small tipi, and a lot of kindling to set beside it. As the sun begins its disappearance behind the mountains, I light the tipi. When I have a good blaze, I pick up one of the small twigs.

Now the ceremony. I think, What do I want to give up, to rid my life of? I answer, my combativeness. When I threw out fundamentalist religion, I got argumentative about it, often with a certain edge. Later the debating turned more to sport, attempts to figure out creative ways to express ideas, or ways to say something memorable or persuasive to the other person. But it was a lousy habit that at best produced nothing and sometimes caused hard feelings.

So now I ask the Powers to take this trait from my life, put a twig on the blaze, and watch it change from wood to light that disappears quickly, to smoke that blows away on the faint breeze, and to heat I can feel on my cheeks. May my combativeness go away so readily.

One by one, I pick up small twigs, think of some inclination of mine that I don't like, some bad habit, some quality that is holding me back or annoying other people, and I repeat the ritual of burning a twig and asking the behavior to go away.

When I get tired of thinking of such things, it is almost dark. I spread out my sleeping bag, lie down on it, and watch the stars. Here at seven thousand feet, a score of miles from even one electric light, I see probably three times as many as I would at sea level near a town. After spotting the north star, I make myself stop identifying constellations and let my mind go blank. Maybe the Powers need a blank slate to write on.

After a while I smoke again and pray again, lie down, and get into the sleeping bag for warmth. I intend to stay awake all night, and look forward especially to a late moonrise. Being cold might make my mind clearer or open my consciousness wider, but...

Unfortunately, the next thing I know the sky is getting light. I missed the moonrise and missed most of the night. But there's no point in berating myself. Back to my ceremonies, smoking the pipe to honor the Powers. singing my gratitude for life and love for the world we live in, and asking for a vision.

In the early afternoon, after a full twenty-four hours at the springs, I give up. Nothing has happened on my first vision quest. As I feared.

I shoulder my pack and start walking out. The rangers suggested whistling so that I wouldn't walk up on a griz without warning. But I don't feel like doing that. Instead I listen to the grouse, who are putting on a show today.

The male grouse, out of sight in the trees but easy to hear, are gathering in what are called leks—little mobs—and doing elaborate courtship dances, grunting out strange, guttural songs, flapping their feathers, and drumming the ground with their wings.

It's entertainment.

So I am listening to a burlesque show when I turn into Saul on the road to Damascus.

As I stroll along blithely, under a clear sky, I see a bolt of lightning knock me down and split my skull. A realization pops up like a huge movie marquee. I push myself to a sitting position on an aching butt in the middle of the trail and look at it:

YOU ARE LIVING YOUR LIFE IN REBELLION.
YOU ARE FIGHTING THE MONSTERS YOU BANNED THIRTY YEARS AGO—FUNDAMENTALISTS, RELIGIOUS CRACKPOTS, NUTTY PEOPLE.
SO THESE ANCIENT ENEMIES ARE RUNNING YOUR LIFE.
INSTEAD OF LETTING THEM GO THEIR WAY,

YOU SPEND TIME AND ENERGY SHOVING BACK AT THEM.
AND THAT'S NOT A LIFE—
BECAUSE THEY'RE RUNNING YOUR SHOW

Holy cow.

I sit on that spot quite a while, repeating the words over and over to myself. I get the message, but I want to remember the words exactly. I'm completely sure of their importance.

Finally I get up and walk on, muttering the marqueed words in rhythm to my steps. I get all the way to the ford without hearing any more grouse, or noticing anything in the forest or the sky.

At the river's edge I sit down for a moment. This is the boundary of the special world I've been in and the ordinary world. I don't expect messages on my windshield on the drive back to Jackson. (On the other hand, I think that *anything* could happen.)

What have I learned?

Well, now I know two ways a vision can come. The first one was like a movie, a short story with characters, dialogue, and action. As in a good movie, the meaning was left to the viewer to grasp. I think of this as the Delphic method.

The other way is a blast about as subtle as the 48-point type newspapers are saving for the end of the world.

NUCLEAR WAR

MOST HUMAN BEINGS DEAD OTHERS DYING

The personal message is more than clear—STOP IT. Now I know I want-want-*want* to change my life, and know something of the path to change.

I look back up the river. I remember the hot springs. The grouse. The lightning. The big-big words.

Take all of it across the river with you. Hold it next to your heart, a treasure every day.

I step into the water. In the middle of the river I sit down in the freezing stuff. *Baptized again!* I think teasingly. The joke is on me.

Later, when I tell Clyde what I saw this time, we both have a good laugh. This one is worth a little talk—I confirm to Clyde that I've been doing just what the marquee said, living in opposition to people and ideas that I rebelled against more than three decades earlier. There are no puzzles here.

Then, seriously—entirely seriously—I take a pledge to make that the first of twelve of such vision quests.

We don't talk any further about what visions are, where they come from, what they mean, and so on. I know they're real. I honor them. I will do what I can to bring other revelations. But I have no idea what will happen, or whether anything will happen. After all, the vision I just finished came after my quest seemed to be over, and in the form of a lightning bolt.

Yeah. I'm sure visions have a heaven of a lot more power than I know. They're like whirling around in the funnel of a tornado—you're silly if you think you can control them.

Crazy Horse, I get it. I get you.

10. WIN, MEET
TASHUNKE WITKO

As I drive home that very day, back to the world where bolts of lightning don't send messages via marquees, I have something else drumming in my mind like a herd of horses. Now I can write the Crazy Horse novel. Fifteen years after I started, blocked by my inability to see the world of a man who ran his life according to visions, I *know* the key to how he saw the world, know by experience, not words in a book, and know I can count on learning more. *This opens the door*, I think, *to ride from the first page to the last*. Then, *This is what it means to see with the single eye of the heart, not the two eyes of the head. And anyone, from Crazy Horse to Clyde to me, would follow whatever Spirit says in that other world. As best as we can understand it.*

I don't know the routes to my goal. I know there are accounts of what Crazy Horse saw in his visions, but they are fragmentary, because he kept a lot of what he saw beyond to himself. His friends and family probably figured some of it out by his behavior. I also don't know how he integrated whatever he saw and heard into day-by-day living. I know it was, well, let's put it mildly and say *distinctive*. His own people called him Our Strange Man. They themselves apparently didn't know what power he got on the mountain, or what Powers he felt especially obliged to honor, or ...

I'm confident that they saw that his spirit animal was Hawk, because it was said that he wore a hawk on his head as he went into battle.

But somehow I feel that what I don't know will manifest itself to me as I write. Don't analyze. Tell what he saw, tell what he did. Follow him to his love of Black Buffalo Woman, to his first fights against the people's ancient enemies, to the skirmishes with the white miners in the Black Hills, to the battles at the Rosebud and the Greasy Grass (Little Big Horn). See who he is, feel who he is, know what he did, and let the dots connect themselves.

A certain faith is called for in writing any novel, and a certain grace asked for. Let it be. In this book, especially, trust the single eye of the heart.

Yes, yes, I'm concerned about one thing—the end of his life. A man I respect so much, admire so much, a man whose life seems to me glorious—how can I let it end as the indisputable facts say it did?

After Crazy Horse gave Custer a whomping defeat at the Little Big Horn, the American armies were truly aroused and determined to make the Lakota people come in and live at the agency. They were to stop hunting buffalo, live on commodities distributed by the government, and eventually learn to settle down and grow crops. In other words, become white people.

To reach that goal, the army interfered with the Lakota's buffalo hunts. That worked so well that in the winter of 1876-77 Crazy Horse's people were on the edge of starvation. Finally Crazy Horse relented and led his people to the agency to get some food right away.

But Crazy Horse himself couldn't stand a life of sitting around with his hand out, hoping for the gift of something to eat. He wanted the old life of hunting, of making his own way, *his* life.

Only when his people were gaunt with starvation did he accept a request from his fellow chiefs to come talk to the agent and the soldiers and work out some compromise.

The invitation turned out to be a trick. To the other chiefs he was not Our Strange Man but The Strange Man. Though the big soldier chief, General Crook, liked Crazy Horse and wanted to be his friend, his enemies among his own people convinced Crook that Crazy Horse had sworn to kill him.

Crook ordered his arrest, and, probably in sorrow, left to go to the railroad.

When Crazy Horse got to the agency, they told him that he could sleep that night and they would have their talk tomorrow. A detachment of policemen from his own people led to his quarters. Which turned out to be a jail.

Crazy Horse knew Hawk couldn't stand imprisonment even for one night. He knew he himself couldn't stand it.

He was a warrior. First, always, a man must be what he is.

So he turned went wild and attacked the policemen with only a knife. They held him while the only white solder present killed him with a bayonet.

I wondered, and still wonder, whether in these fateful moments he thought this fate was what he had seen in his first vision two decades earlier. In that seeing beyond he was impervious to the white man's bullets, but the hands of his people held him back, and it was not a bullet that killed him.

Regardless, the whole event seemed to me ignominious. A great man brought down by the classic excuse, "killed while trying to escape."

To me his death should somehow have been a transfiguration, a sacrifice that brought a tidal wave of blessing, touched with a kind of glory.

But I did not see how. Not yet.

So I set to work. First, I wanted to know much more about Lakota customs and daily life. I wanted to know everything, down to what the women used in the cradleboards to keep babies dry. Clyde could tell me a lot. I'd been to the Pine Ridge and Sicangu reservations repeatedly, knew some people there, and was in touch with some members of the Crazy Horse family. (He had no direct descendants.) But I wanted more. Fortunately, I had discovered that if I approached Lakota people with a good heart, they would see my heart and talk to me. And I wanted more familiarity with their ways, much more familiarity.

Comment: The last words of every Lakota prayer, and every Lakota ceremony, are "*Mitaku oyasin.*" They mean, "We are all related."

Absorb that. I am related to you, and you to me. You are also related to all your family, and friends, and neighbors. And the people you work with, the people you drive the freeway or ride the subway with. And in fact to all living beings.

We are all related. If I want know how you feel when you hold your newborn child for the first time, I need only go to the place in myself that remembers the same experience, or talk to several mothers about how it felt, or use the empathy we are all born with. If I want to know how you feel after getting divorced, the same. We are all human beings—black, white, Polynesian, Mexican, Cherokee, Irish ... In fact, all the two-legged, the four-legged, the winged, the crawlers, those with fins, those with roots, and far more—the stone people, the wind people, the waters, the soil of Mother Earth—to all the world I say, "*Mitaku oyasin.*"

The quantum physicists go further. They see all things centrally as bundles of energy, particles whirling around atoms. But I leave that to them.

46

Meanwhile, in writing this book, I developed a strong conviction about the meaning of the words "we are all related." They mean that we can understand each other through empathy, a crucial human capacity. Sometimes we don't have to be told how something feels—we know by looking inside ourselves.

Also, because we are all related, _Mitaku oyasin,_ the fitting response to the existence of all other human beings, and all living beings, is compassion. We are alike. We should feel for each other. We _can_ know how other people feel.

So, for the purpose of writing my book about Crazy Horse, I worked from a strong feeling of being related by blood and cell to Crazy Horse, to his best friend Hump, to his favorite uncle Spotted Tail, and everyone else in his life.

No Lakota person has ever asked me how I can write about them. They know we are all related.

In all my books, and all through my life, I stand on the conviction that we are all related. For me, that is a way of soaring.

Back then in 1991, I launched into writing like a river in spring run-off. When you walk a path you don't know, you can't see beyond the next turn. You can't anticipate the desert you'll have to cross, the river you'll have to wade, the mountain ridge you must climb.

You can't know whether the journey will be worthwhile.

But you can relish every hour of it.

You have some urges or feelings, some warmth in the blood, some pulse within that says, "Go." If you're a writer who has walked this path before, if you're willing to let your creativity run free, you go like a madman, galloping into the unknown. In that way you end up somewhere you've never been.

The key is to look with the single eye of the heart. Write not with your brain but your whole self—yes, your thoughts, but also your senses, your memory, your imagination, your emotions, the pump of your blood, the experience of your skin, the knowledge of your soul—the awareness of all you, the whole person.

With that commitment to seeing with the single eye of the heart I went forward from the day I waded across the river from the ordinary world to the extraordinary and saw with the single of eye of my heart.

And I knew there was much, much more to see.

11. WHEN THE STUDENT IS READY, THE TEACHER WILL APPEAR

During the year after my vision, I devoted myself to understanding the early years of the life of Tashunke Witko and to setting down what I learned and shaping it in a way that felt true to his spirit.

I had a good situation. On our property in Jackson was a one-room cabin I used as my writer's hideaway. It was full of books, two pet ferrets, long hours of work, a waste can stuffed with pages that seemed not beautiful enough, and a multitude of grand ideas. I imagined, I sketched, I wrote trial pages, and wrote better pages. I shared a life with the youth who had hair and skin the color of river sand and had not yet blossomed into Tashunke Witko, He Whose Horse Dance in a Sacred Manner.

That fall a tall, handsome Brulé Sioux came to Jackson to give a speech. I was tremendously impressed by his attitudes, by his wisdom, and most of all by the palpable goodness of his heart.

When his speech ended, I introduced myself to Joseph Marshall III, and told him I was writing a novel about the life of Crazy Horse. And told him more than that, exposing my feelings.

He said, "Now I know why I came to Jackson Hole. I came to meet you."

Joe and I went out and drank coffee and talked. I asked questions. He asked questions. We batted ideas around. He gave me information and insights I had gotten only a whiff of. And when we said good night, we had an agreement that he would consult with me every step of the way on the book, read every page, and help me to enter into the Lakota world more fully.

I didn't understand until the end of the process how lucky I was to have Joe. First, he is what is called a grandfather's child, an eldest son taken into a remote region of the reservation from birth and kept away from everything Anglo. As a small child Joe never rode in a car, never heard a radio or saw a television set, never went to a convenience store, never talked to a white person. He lived in the old way.

His transition into American culture later was difficult, but irrelevant here. He ended up going to college, teaching in college, and even writing books—he has a baker's dozen published now, and they are acclaimed.

But what I treasure him for is helping me give birth to my incarnation of Tashunke Witko in words. When the manuscript was finished and about to be published, Joe even suggested that I come to his house and go into his sweat lodge with him, so that we could ask together for the help of the spirits with the launching of the book. When the novel won honors, his response was, "I expected that."

I will talk to him about this book as well.

On the adventure, sometimes you meet enemies, sometimes guides.

I know well that Joe, Clyde, my own passion to understand, and the Powers winged me up high for the writing of that book. And the Powers spoke particularly on my vision quest the next autumn.

I start by going back to the place I love, Snake River Hot Springs, spend the afternoon in the prescribed sacred manner, performing the ceremony of burning twigs that represent things that I want to get out of my life, and in the twilight I walk a little along the trail that winds up toward a ridge. I quickly find what I'm looking for, a pine tree that leans back at the base. It will make a comfortable prop for my back during the night, and I think sitting up will help me stay awake.

First I lean against the tree and listen to my animal friends being very noisy. (*Mitaku oyasin.*) The elk are frolicking through their annual autumn rut, and the most conspicuous part of that is their bugling. The males emit blasts of trumpet-like sounds intended to establish dominance over other males and attract females. These blasts are as rowdy as shouts on the floor of a huge stock exchange, except that the bulls are on the prowl for sex, not profit.

I am also listening to something surprising, which has been going on for an hour or two. Wolves are howling in the valley beyond the ridge.

There's no mistaking a wolf's howl for a coyote's cry. Wolves h0-O-O-Owl. Coyotes go yip-yip-YIP, yip-YIP. A difference like the one between hearing the roar of lions and the playful cries of children.

The howl is a lovely sound. I always think of it as a welcome to the moon, so far away and yet so bright.

What really gives me a kick about these particular howls, though, is that there are no wolves in Yellowstone Park—or so the park officials tell us. These folk are having meetings (the one talent of bureaucrats) about re-introducing the wolf "soon." The last ones in the park were killed in 1926, and maybe…

What a hoot (pun intended). The wolves are already here—they've reintroduced themselves. They're not waiting for permission. Tonight they're already calling, "Howlelujah!"

I am as thrilled as I would have been at a concert of a great symphony by a great orchestra. Or, since this music is illicit, more thrilled.

Propped against the tree, as twilight surrenders to darkness, I enjoy the elk-wolf orchestra.

After a while I hear something coming down the trail from the ridge above. The darkness is absolute now, and my back is to the trail, but I know what it is. An elk. Cloppety-clop. Yes, an elk. I wish he'd bugle, but his nose is telling him I'm not a lady elk, so…

No, wait. I'm mistaken. It's not an elk, or even a clop-clop. That's the footpad of a bear.

Oh well, I'm not worried about grizzlies. They're people-shy, really people-shy. Let him come, let him pass, enjoy…

Wait. No, I'm mistaken again. That sound isn't a pad, it *is* a clop, and…

Damn, it's a moose. (Somehow I know for sure what each animal is.) Damn it. Moose are opposite of people-shy. They will attack. They will go on a rampage of hoof-beating. Damn it!

I slide down, my back to the moose. Maybe he won't see or smell…

Wait. Hell, I'm mistaken again. That's no moose. What's wrong with me? That's a wolf. No question—listen to those velvety paws on the trail.

I'm not afraid of the wolf—I'm glad to hear him, and wolves don't bother people.

I'm getting spooked, though, by the mysterious goings-on. They don't make sense.

The wolf steps off the trail and pads toward me.

I huddle down further.

He comes right up to me. Or she comes to me.

She stands over my head for a moment—I can feel her breath.

Then she nuzzles my neck.

If I weren't frozen into stone, I might claw my way up the tree. Instead I'm as still as a marble statue.

In a moment the wolf is gone. I didn't hear her walk away—she evaporated.

I decide not to move for the rest of the night.

I don't realize how foolish I've been until morning. That was no literal, this-world parade of exactly four animals passing by me, nor was the wolf's touch physical, and it was no accident.

That was all a vision. I saw beyond. My visitors were not an elk, a bear, a moose, and a wolf—these honoraries were Elk, Bear, Moose, and Wolf in their eternal forms.

It's embarrassing to realize that I had thought, at the time and all night long (you think I could *sleep* after that?), that four physical animals had walked along the trail, three had passed me by, and one had nosed me before moving along.

This morning I try not to think about it. I build a fire, warm myself up, and smoke my pipe. "*Pila maya,* Tunkashila." 'Thank you, Grandfathers.' The words are nervous. I haven't recovered from last night's uncanny event yet.

Then I use what I remember from books and the stories of Lakota people and figure it out. I was wide awake—no way to pretend it was a dream. And the procession of the animals was ceremonial. In fact, it had a lot in common with the great story of White Buffalo Calf Woman.

Many grasses and many snows ago, when the people were starving, White Buffalo Calf Woman came to them. She wore the skin of a deer so white it gleamed in the sun, so they knew she was *wakan*, holy.

She brought them the greatest of gifts, the sacred pipe, with its red bowl symbolizing Mother Earth and its stem symbolizing all things that grow on our Mother, and she taught them how to smoke the sacred tobacco.

That pipe is the greatest treasure of the Lakota people even today, and the keeper of that pipe, Arvol Looking Horse, is the latest of a long tradition of hosts of this holy relic.

What matters to me now, though, is how White Buffalo Calf Woman departed. Walking away, she rolled over and turned into a black buffalo, then walked, rolled over, and turned into a brown buffalo, then a red buffalo, and last a white buffalo calf.

Four animals came to me in a similar way, four, walking toward me rather than away from me. They were not just different colors, they were different animals. And over the years the wolf has given me gifts.

But right now, back still against the tree, I am stupefied. Wide awake. Entirely "rational" and aware of the "real" world. A vision in which nothing appeared to my sense of sight, but only to my hearing and my senses of touch and smell. And a vision I understand *not at all*, and feel I will never understand.

Yet I know it's a gift.

I smoke my pipe again and give much more heartfelt gratitude, *Pila Maya, Tunkashila,* not in the sense of the father of my father, but our Grandfather who is *wakan*.

Then I sing some songs in English, and finally several I improvise. I have never improvised musically before, but it feels great.

And when the sun is high, I walk back into the "real" world.

Back at the car something comical but educational happened.

I passed the ranger station, got to the highway, and sat down on the curb between my car and the big sign announcing YELLOWSTONE NATIONAL PARK.

It's hard to explain this. I was having trouble adjusting to our culture's "reality" after what I had seen beyond. Cars whizzing by and rangers in a box doing paperwork seemed absurd and utterly trivial. I could not accept those doings as "real."

What was this odd, unimportant world? Clyde had said it is an illusion, and the real world is beyond. Yes, that's right.

I wasn't ready to get into my car, whatever a car was, and drive back to town, whatever a town was. What waited there did not feel like my true home.

12. WHAT A
GREAT GIFT!

I went to see Clyde, and we went back into the sweat lodge, the proper place to tell a man of wisdom what you saw on the mountain and to thank the Powers for it.

Clyde listened attentively to my description of hearing the elk and wolves all afternoon, and the visits, one by one, of the four animals that night.

He said almost casually, "Of course, it means the wolf is your spirit animal."

An electric shock ran up my spine from my bottom and exploded in my head.

I have been given a spirit animal.

What greater gift could I have asked for? What greater blessing could I have received?

Yet I did not immediately think of the wolf as like me. He is the patron of war and the hunt.

Back at home I researched wolves. In their real behavior in the world, they fight no wars and hunt only as a group, in a distinctly cooperative way, and only for food. They are devoted family (pack) animals.

(Yes, they feed on other living beings. Every living thing on this planet lives by consuming life. With each breath we consume living beings.)

Wolves find a creature that looks vulnerable, perhaps a fawn or an elk calf. Working together, they bring it down. Two wolves chase the target hard, wearing it down. Along the way they communicate by body language—movements of the hair and ear, body posture, facial expressions. They also yelp, howl, whine, and growl as signals. Then they peel off, and two other wolves chase the victim hard again. This goes on by turns until they wear out their prey and bring it down.

Wolves are very much team players, and have a definite order among themselves. The leaders are a mating pair, and one of them is the alpha wolf. First among their soldiers are their adult offspring, who do not mate. Then come the juveniles, and last the cubs.

They are a tight-knit family. *Lone wolf* is a nonsense term.

I thought of myself as a family man, but not in the kind of family I wanted. We were two adults and a ten-year-boy. I felt very close to my son, Ethan, but not to my wife. Our marriage was best described as civility, silence, and distance.

For the moment I sought something to make me think every day of wolf, something I could touch and in that feel his comradeship. A Shoshone friend of Clyde's traded me a wolf claw.

When I asked a local jeweler to make a silver cap for it, he said, "It's ceremonial, isn't it? Wolf is your spirit animal."

I was taken aback. I had never met this man before, and as far as I knew, he had no idea who I was. But I said yes.

"In that case, I'll do the job free."

Marvelous. And only in a part of the West near Indian people would that have been recognized.

When I picked up the capped claw, this stranger also gave me a silver chain for hanging it around my neck.

On the road we sometimes meet enemies, sometimes helpers.

I wore it for ten years, and rubbed it often, until I went into the hospital for a couple of weeks and it disappeared. I don't know whether a nurse took it or it just came undone and got carried off with the dirty sheets.

I'm asking an old friend for better wolf totem right now.

I looked up the meaning of the word "Blevins" in Welsh. It means wolf.

For the next three years I lived an intensely focused life. I made breakfast for myself and my ten-year-old son, Ethan. I took him to school. Then I sat at my computer and wrote, my body in the small writing cabin but my soul walking with Crazy Horse in a world a century past.

At three o'clock I picked Ethan up from school, did errands, cooked dinner, waited to see how soon my wife the doctor would finish with rounds at the hospital. Then we ate, I played with Ethan or watched television with him, told him a bedtime story—he never let me get by without making up a new story, always about Jellystone Park—and the next morning I went back to the exhilaration of living in Crazy Horse's world.

My marriage? Brittle. Stiff. A little distant.

My fatherhood? Warm, satisfying.

My imaginary companionship with Tashunke Witko?

Like a creek charging down a mountain, th0se waters were wild and exhilarating.

In this way were my days split like chunks of firewood between the world of everyday experience and the world of imagination.

Since I was imagining, feeling, and rendering the experiences of Tashunke Witko into words, I often said to him, "Pila Maya, Grandfather." Meaning "Thank you."

Writing is adventuring, especially writing fiction. That summer I met an editor at a writer's conference, Robert Gleason of TOR, who believed he could get a renaissance of writing about the West going. He talked a good game, so I told him about my book about Crazy Horse.

"A biography?" he wanted to know.

"A biographical novel," I said, "completely accurate—creative non-fiction." That genre, pioneered by Truman Capote, Tom Wolfe, and others, was still not completely accepted.

"Why not a biography?"

"Two reasons. We don't know enough facts to write a solid historical account of his life. The story would be full of holes, and the information wouldn't have the environment that gives it meaning. And the big reason is, I want go into his mind, tell his thoughts, sing his feelings." I let a beat go by. "Facts aren't truth. They're skeletons that need flesh, a heart, and spirit to become truth."

He accepted that and we signed a contract, my best up to that time. For me it was as sacred as a bidding from King Arthur to a knight. At last I was given orders to ride into the dark forest, where no man had gone, find a book that was full of Spirit, and bring it forth.

On December 29, 1990 I drove with Terry, a writer friend, to Wounded Knee for the hundred-year memorial for the deaths of most of Big Foot's people. On my previous visit there I'd felt tremendous pain—Clyde said it was the pain of Big Foot's people, who died there.

Now I was keen to see, hear, and feel the ceremony Wiping Away of the Tears. After a century the medicine men would perform that ceremony to heal the damage of that awful bloodletting. The ceremony could be performed only once every seven generations, the Lakota expression for a hundred years. If it failed, the pain would endure for another century.

Terry and I walked up the hill toward the church and stopped at the mass grave site again. It seemed to me that the human beings buried there were restless, crying out.

I looked around and studied the reality of what I'd only read about in books. On the flat just down the hill the men of the tribe sat in council with the army officers, surrounded by the riflemen of Custer's old outfit, the Seventh Cavalry. The soldiers took away the Big Foot men's rifles. To the army's thinking, this was forcing them to be peaceful. In the Indians' mind it meant they would have no way to hunt, and their people were already gaunt from hunger. Searching for even more rifles, soldiers rummaged through the blankets of the men at the council by force, and when dissatisfied went to the village and searched the tipis.

I remembered the wonderful cry from one of the older men during this demeaning treatment, a dire threat to the tribe for the three months of winter ahead. This man stood up and made an appeal for human decency. He bellowed, "We are a people in the world!"

His words were blown away in the wind.

Off to my right was the open field where the tipis had been put up on that day, where the women were cooking or doing other domestic tasks and the children were playing their games and chasing the dogs—a typical village scene.

On the hill where Terry and I stood the Hotchkiss guns had been stationed, surprisingly close to the village. When the first shots were fired at the council circle, these guns raked the tipis with machine-gun fire, killing women, children, dogs, and even decimating the dolls the children were playing with.

Looking back, even now I can barely speak of my feelings.

The physical sensations are easy. It was thirty degrees below zero, which is acutely painful. As we looked at the mass grave, I saw a tear leak from Terry's eye. After sliding a quarter inch downward, the drop froze solid.

We spent a lot of the time inside the church, drinking hot coffee, not so much warming our flesh as relieving the sharp pains in our hearts.

Outside we stood among hundreds of people, Lakota by a large majority, gathered there for the great task of that day, the ceremony of healing.

Everyone knew how much the tears needed wiping away. To the Lakota people the killing here was no event of the remote past. The wounds were still open and bleeding. Many people present right then had ancestors who had died on that day, ancestors who should have been part of their lives as grandparents but were not. That included women and children who had fled several miles before some galloping soldier lopped off a head with his sabre. Why would anyone whack the head of a woman or a child far from the fighting and fleeing the scene?

The injuries and deaths of ancestors here, these were the flames of family tales, often recounted, handed down from generation to generation in pain, often in anger.

Later an editor at my publishing house asked me, "But why does it matter now? It's so far in the past."

Because of his question I wrote a novel called *RavenShadow* about Joseph Blue Crow, a man who was raised by his grandmother, who was given birth by a mother dying in the bed of Wounded Knee Creek. Because of his upbringing, the blood of Wounded Knee ran in Blue's veins. And because his grandmother's life was mangled on that day, she passed on twisted and tortured emotions to him.

Blue was in hot water, drinking too much, unemployed, recently divorced.

In the novel Blue comes to this killing ground on this day. Here he is given a vision, and in it he travels back a hundred years and sees every detail of his grandmother's pain, and he sees as well the deaths of his grandmother and grandfather. In that way he comes to know the burdens he has been carrying, unaware.

Blue uses his new understanding to rediscover the good red road.

Other Lakota people, right here in front of me, were surely in struggles liked Blue's. I hoped they would find healing.

Suddenly came a beautiful event. The Big Foot Memorial Riders had ridden, wagoned, and walked for the last five years consecutively along the route of the Big Foot band. Those people of a hundred years ago had intended to join their relatives at Fort Robinson and get the commodities promised them by treaty. But they were stopped a few miles from safety on these barren hills along Wounded Knee Creek.

Here, now, came the Big Foot Memorial riders again. In the dress of their ancestors, they circled the mass grave and brought their mounts to attention facing it.

It was a heart-stirring sight. I will never forget the silhouettes of the riders, nor stop thinking of their sacrifice, riding day after day in those terrible temperatures.

That afternoon Terry and I went to the Wiping of the Tears ceremony at a local high school, and I met several Lakota men who talked to me about the meaning of this event, and the legacy of Wounded Knee. Our shared grief built bridges.

A sad day but a good one.

More sad when one of the men I'd met there told me later that the medicine men said the ceremony hadn't worked. The tears had not been wiped away. Now the people would live with that horror for seven more generations.

A day like that feels awful and awesome at once. I was up to my eyeballs in compassion. I was not thinking only of those Lakotas, but of the peoples who have told tales of that kind of suffering since human beings first gathered around fires to speak their truth.

Human nature is often difficult to fathom, and evil is forever an impenetrable mystery.

In spite of the failure of the ceremony, there is a lot to be grateful for in that day. The Big Foot Memorial Riders are still riding. They started out with the intention of riding five times, with a climax in 1990, the actual hundredth anniversary. As I write, in the past December they completed the twenty-fifth anniversary of the 1990 ride. I echo what the descendants of the victims of the Holocaust say—"Never forget."

The Bigfoot Memorial Riders

13. SOARING AND SOARING

M. Scott Peck, a psychiatrist who published a several popular self-help books in the '70s and '80s, wrote that when he graduated from medical school, a newly branded M.D., he held to the scientific viewpoint—there are no miracles—everything has a natural explanation. Decades later, he said, he believes the opposite. Everything is a miracle.

I side with his second self. I see the earth itself as a single living organism. A vast energy animates every cell of it—in all human beings, all four-legged creatures, all the winged, all the crawlers, all the rooted, all the soil, the sand, the stone, the water, the sky, the moon, the sun—every molecule of this is a manifestation of the miracle of that energy, which may be called Spirit, or *taku skan skan.*

Those last words came from Joe Marshall. Once, after many conversations and deepening trust, I dared to ask him the essence of Lakota spirituality.

He said that before the Lakota people were influenced by Christianity, they called the Ultimate Power *taku skan skan.* Then he translated those words as "that which moves that which moves."

I exclaimed, "Energy!" That stood for a while. Later Joe said, "It means the life force on the planet."

Good. I understand. Above all I love the force of life itself on Earth. All living beings. *Mitaku oyasin*—we are all related, truly.

Right on, Dr. Peck. *Everything* is truly a miracle. And to know that everything on earth is a miracle, including human beings, is to love it all.

And with that understanding I felt that I had reached fully my goal of many years ago: Spiritually, I was *soaring*.

14. AN EAGLE SOARS, CRAZY HORSE SOARS, AND I JOIN THEM

In ways that are hard to express, after going to Wounded Knee in December 0f 1992, I was a changed man. I was at home with my awareness of the world beyond. That affected my gait on my daily walk, the way I looked at the sky, the way the earth smelled, my pleasure in watching the sparrowhawks and the magpies, my feelings of good will toward everyone I encountered, my love of the earth, the universe, and everyone and everything within it.

Such is the man who now hikes up the Snake River each October, heading for the hot springs, the home of my vision quests. Oddly, this time I decide to forego getting a permit to use the campground from the rangers.

My mind is very much elsewhere. For fifteen years I have been writing what I see as my finest book, my tale of the life of Crazy Horse. For years I haven't been able to see how I can describe his death, because it seems to me ignominious, unworthy of him. He was tricked into being escorted by soldiers of his own people to a cabin where he could sleep. When he realized that it was a jail, he knew that his spirit could not bear being locked up even for a night. Neither could his spirit animal, Hawk.

Against impossible odds, he fought the Indian soldiers with only a knife—and got bayoneted fatally by the only white soldier there.

Unacceptable, to me. An absurd cliché—killed while trying to escape. Ignominious.

I walk into the clearing where the springs are and see—ouch!—that the campground is occupied. Maybe I should have asked the rangers for a permit.

Oh, never mind, the trail goes on, and there will be another campground somewhere ahead. Why not see a little more of this spectacular country?

The only real change is that the main trail now leads across the river, and the water looks deeper than at the south entrance ford I'm accustomed to.

Straight ahead—wade in. It's briskly cold, but no more than that. Soon it gets thigh high, even crotch high, and I'm glad of the pebbly footing.

In midstream I look upriver and—wow! —a bald eagle is flying straight toward me. The country has lots of them, but this one is different. It seems to be gliding on a path that will bring it directly over my head, and no more than fifteen feet above me. I have never seen anything like this.

I stand transfixed. Right over me the eagle flies, cruising, not wing-flapping. About twenty yards downstream it begins to flap its wings, and goes into a gentle curve to the left, and after another twenty yards a curve back to the right, and after twenty more yards comes turn back to the center line. Now it goes back to gliding, its course straight downriver. The eagle has written a perfect S in the sky and sailed on.

As I gape at the bird, images drop into my head like earth from a dump truck. After worrying for years about the ending of *Stone*

Song, I suddenly see it all as a movie, shot by shot, full of feeling. I could write the music that accompanies it. And it is perfect, everything I want.

Sometimes come messengers.

I push ahead as fast as I can against the current. I want urgently to get to the far bank and write down what I have seen in my head.

Quickly, I climb out onto the sand, flop down, throw my backpack down, and out of the zipper pocket in the top flap take my stenographer's notebook and a ballpoint. I always carry these, in case there are words I want to remember. Now I'm going to scribble this gift onto paper while it's still hot in me.

I let my mind see the images and hear the sounds again and write them down. In six or eight minutes I am finished.

I had worried that Crazy Horse's death would seem an ugly murder and a stomach-churning tragedy, spoiling the glory that was his life.

Now it feels like a transfiguration.

In fact, it's so good that I intend to type it straight into the manuscript, unchanged. And those words stand today, unchanged, the last two pages of the book, just as the eagle brought me the story. Here they are:

> A jumble. Pain like a huge wave boiling. A room. The *wasicu* doctor, a needle going into his arm, a strange unreality, pleasant and ugly, like a sour vision. The murmurings of his father, Worm, his mothers, his uncle Touch the Sky.
>
> Through it all Hawk was quiet, still, at peace.
>
> More jumble: Lifting on the wave of pain. Doctor. Tears and lamentations. Cresting on the wave of pain. Vague and intermittent drumbeats. Floating, washing toward death. Tonight his spirit, the one known to him as Hawk, would go beyond the pines. His heart flooded with warmth from Wi, the sun.

Tonight the single eye of his heart would close and his spirit would go to live beyond the pines.

His father wept. His mothers and uncle wept.

He yearned to go.

He tried to speak to them. "*He, he, he,*" he tried to say, he tried to say. Regret, regret, regret.

Hawk felt the wind in her face. She turned into it, and felt its lift. Power, power, the wind has power.

Gently, she raised her wings and rose a little. She hovered. The wind was from the north, and she understood, understood not in words, but in a change in her breast. The wind was growing colder. Yes, it was from the north. She would fly that direction, and on beyond the pines. She would not see the sun rise again.

She rose a little on the wind, feeling its strength. She felt a wish to hover over this small cabin huddled in the darkness. She heard the human beings wailing, singing one of the great songs of their kind, a song of grief.

It was almost time, but not yet. An awareness held her like a falconer's will, a connection with the man below, a beat.

She rode the wind there in the darkness, waiting.

It came simply. She felt a tug in her breast. It hurt a little, and she knew that the single eye below was closed, and the drum was silent.

She felt her freedom. It was time to fly.

Hawk mounted on the wind a little and turned to the west. She circled the cabin four times, sunwise. The first time she hovered for a moment in the west, where the Wakinyan dwell. The second time in the north, where the White Giant lives. The third time in the east, home of the sun. Last she faced the south, the giver of life, as a salute.

She turned slowly back to the north and felt a thrill at the strength of the wind. She mounted higher and higher into the sky in great rings made sunwise, higher and higher. When she would have been beyond the sight of human beings even in daylight, she turned for the last time into the north wind, flapped her wings, and began her journey.

Before the sun rose on this earth she would be soaring beyond the pines at the edge of the world, beyond the path of the winds, away in the northern sky where there is no darkness, no sickness or sorrow of any kind can come, and the spirits swell in peace and beauty.

Those scribblings in my notebook gave me the conclusion to my book I had I longed for, but I still had about a hundred earlier pages left to write, out of more than four hundred.

The eagle had brought wonders—the remaining pages gushed out of me like a spring flood through a culvert. I could hardly keep up with the surge. Every day I sat down, turned on the computer, got the file up, pumped a fist into the air, and yelled "Sock it to me, Jesus!" And yelled it again during the writing day.

I finished that draft between Thanksgiving and Christmas, sent it to Joe Marshall, and he added invaluable notes. About the first day of spring I had a manuscript that seemed to me to gleam.

I sent it to the new editor assigned to me by the house (that first fellow had proved to be an ass), and Harriet McDougal turned out to be the best editor I ever had. She loved the manuscript I sent. It was accepted, which meant the second half of the advance would be on the way. And she promised to rouse the full enthusiasm of the publishing house behind the book.

Soon one of the publicists at the publishing house called me to tell that the publisher was nominating the book for the Pulitzer Prize.

That was euphoria, but a more extraordinary, seemingly miraculous moment was ahead.

And where did it come to me?

Where else? At Wounded Knee.

15. A SACRED DANCE

On the very week of publication of *Stone Song*, a timing that seemed very propitious, I went with Lakota and Anglo friends to this shrine. Yes, it had come to feel like a shrine to me. And we would be attending the sun dance.

Since this was my first time at a sun dance, there was a lot to take in. My reading had given me a head start, and my friends helped a lot, but seeing, smelling, and hearing meant a lot more.

The dancers had spent a lot of time preparing for the ceremony. They'd rebuilt the arbor that surrounded the dance ground, to give shade to those of us who were part of the ceremony but not actually dancing. Led by a medicine man, they'd found the sacred tree and erected it in the middle of the circle. The tree was bright with flags representing the powers of the four winds, red for east, yellow for south, black for west, and white for north. They'd attached leather ropes to the tree, to be used in a blood sacrifice during the dance. They'd built sweat lodges and brought plenty of rocks to heat in the fires, and had purified themselves in the steam and with the songs and prayers customary to the sweat lodge.

The ceremony consists of five days of dancing and gazing at the sun, singing, letting the body respond to the beat of the drum, and all the while neither eating nor drinking. To say the least, it is physically demanding.

Not only the dancers were participants in the sun dance. The relatives, friends, and guests sitting in the arbor, observing—they were supporting the dancers with their prayers. They were giving energy and in return getting the ceremony's blessings. Fortunately, that included me.

The most surprising part of the sun dance is the piercing, the blood sacrifice to the Powers. Since I later was pierced myself, I can describe it accurately.

The dancer lies flat on his back. A medicine man kneels next to him with a scalpel that hasn't been used before (this is a new development, due to AIDS) and makes two sets of two parallel cuts about an inch long between the collarbone and the nipple of the dancer and on each side of the sternum. Then he slips pieces of bone or wood beneath the skin so that both ends stick out, takes one of the leather ropes tied to the sacred tree, and ties its V-shaped end to the pieces of wood or bone that jut out. (If the dancer is a woman, which is uncommon but acceptable, the cuts are made in the skin of the shoulders.)

Then the supplicant dances toward the tree, backs away from it, and when the rope grows taut, throws himself backwards, breaking free by tearing his skin. Blood streams down his chest.

Variations are possible. Some experienced dancers may increase the intensity of their sacrifice by leaning back against the rope, but not hard enough to break free. That makes the skin stretch outward for several inches around the cuts, which looks very painful.

At this dance one man leaned back against the tension on his rope for several minutes. His chest skin tented out from his collarbone to his diaphragm. Onlookers in the arbor oohed and aahed. This was a *big* sacrifice for whatever the dancer was asking, for himself or perhaps for the Lakota people as a whole, or all the people of the world. We would never know his exact wish, but we were awestruck.

And then Spirit brought an astounding gift to me.

Immediately after his blood sacrifice, a dancer's sacred pipe is imbued with special power, and he is enabled to take this pipe to someone else and let them make one request of this powerful pipe.

This young man brought his pipe straight to me.

I was astonished. I was one of perhaps five Anglos among two or three hundred Lakota people. He could not possibly have known me. I had only two or three acquaintances locally. How did this man choose me for such an extraordinary gift? And why?

He said, "If you accept this pipe, it will give you whatever you ask for."

I was stunned. The pipe was invested at this moment with this dancer's remarkable sacrifice. And he was willing to give me that medicine, which was unparalleled in this sun dance.

My mind whirled. Then I told myself calmly, *Don't ask for anything for yourself. Ask for something larger.* But I couldn't think of what.

I said, "I'm not ready. Would you bring the pipe back tomorrow?

An outrageous request, but he said yes. And in fact he did bring it back.

I took the pipe, held it high, and said, "I pray with this pipe that my book *Stone Song* will change a million hearts." And handed the pipe back to him with profound thanks.

I have never seen him again. No one I knew spoke to me about his gesture or his name, or why, out of a couple of hundred people, he chose me for that gift.

It felt to me like a blessing of the Grandfather Spirit, Tunkashila, acting through this man.

Today, after two decades, I would make the same request of Tunkashila. Though the book has sold a lot of copies and gone into a lot of libraries, I can only hope that it has changed a million hearts.

If it has not, I ask Spirit here and now, in these words, to charge forward with that process: Let *Stone Song* change a million hearts.

If it has already changed that many, I ask Spirit to help the book change ten million hearts.

Two young Lakota men leaning back against the ropes tied to
the sacred tree (youtube.com)

16. A NEW
CEREMONIAL LIFE

In the end I present myself to you as a typical man, a person who struggles to live up to his best perceptions of himself and of the possibilities of living on this earth, and fails on some days and succeeds on others.

My experience with visions at the Snake River Hot Springs were not just good—they were spectacular. One year I got the great gift of a spirit animal, and the next year a truly amazing gift—the climactic pages of the book I'd been working on for years, my account of the life of Crazy Horse. A chapter in my life had been completed, and Spirit had been generous to me in ways I would not have dared to hope for.

Time for a next step: Clyde had started an annual ceremony at St. John the Divine in New York, a revival of the Shoshone people's Naraya dance. He spoke to me gently about considering coming to the dance. (Native people generally make their guidance gentle.)

I was nearly penniless because of being in the midst of a painful divorce, so it took some putting together. I had a friend who was also going to the dance, and I traded her a Hopi carving of a white buffalo kachina for a plane ticket. The organizers of the dance let me participate free (starving artist status can be a help), and Clyde arranged for the matriarch of a famously rich American family—let's call her Juliette—to give me a place to stay before and after, in her elegant upper Fifth Avenue apartment. It was filled with the art of a true collector, everything from folk art of South America to a Picasso, yet not extravagant or showy for a person of her means. She gives a lot of time and energy to Native causes—she's a marvelous woman.

The Naraya dance, which has continued for three decades and is now called the Dance for All Peoples, is a grandchild of the vision of Wovoka, the Paiute prophet. which swept across the northern Rockies and Plains during the 1880s. Clyde has revived it and its songs and made of it a dance for all spiritual seekers. Participants learn the songs during the day and then dance all night in a great circle holding hands.

An experienced friend told me, "At that dance Spirit is going to kick your ass." I had no idea what she meant, but I found out.

I hesitate to describe it in detail. The door of St. John the Divine closed on Friday evening and didn't reopen until dawn Monday morning. First we spent all of one day learning traditional songs in the Shoshone and Lakota languages. Early in Saturday evening we had our faces painted and dressed for the dance. From mid evening through a long night, we gave ourselves wholly to dancing and singing.

From the start I felt like we had been transported to another world. Clyde led his helpers into the darkened room, dressed traditionally and blowing calls to Spirit on their eagle bone whistles. The effect was eerie, beautiful, hypnotic, and lifted my spirit into an indescribable state of consciousness.

We dancers, about eighty of us, formed a circle around the Tree of Life, which the helpers had dug up and put in the middle of the big room. Holding hands, we did a simple shuffle step clockwise and sang the first song. Any song might be repeated several times. Clyde let Spirit guide him to know when to let each song end and plunge into the next.

From the start some dancers fell down and cried out. I'd been told that dancers often had visions, and helpers were there for them. People having visions cross into the world beyond, and may need contact with this world to help them come back.

Some of the songs were extraordinarily beautiful. One of my two favorites was a Lakota Eagle song, but it is forbidden to sing it outside the Naraya, so I will not write down any of the words or the name of the man who created it. Toward the end of the dance the songs became ethereal and gave forth a feeling that we were approaching the other world in a beautiful and sacred way.

Though I had had several visions, for some reason I didn't think they would come to me in this context. The beauty of everything was mesmeric, but that first night I saw nothing.

On the second night, without warning, I began to see. I did not fall down, and had no impulse to do that. While I saw, I kept dancing and gave no indication that anything extraordinary was happening.

Yet it was amazing. I saw myself as a painter and artist in stained glass. I was living in Greenwich Village in the 1920s. This was surprising partly because, though I work deftly with words and in music, I thought I had no talent in the visual arts.

Yet here I was thumbing through paintings in my own portfolio. The paintings were Manhattan street scenes and showed the influence of Edward Hopper's dark café canvases. The paintings were good, damned good. I can still see one, the canopied entrance to a hospital lit to aid night entry. It's clear enough in my mind that if I had the skill to paint in this ordinary state of mind today, even now I could make a copy of the painting I saw.

But what I really liked was my creations in stained glass. I saw these works as an integral part of the sacred spirit of churches and cathedrals. They were primarily clear, green, silver, and purple, and had purely abstract designs, no saints or saviors included. They had lots of diamond shapes and some half circles. I loved them and immediately wanted to start doing stained glass.

After a while the scene simply disappeared, and I kept dancing as though nothing had happened.

I told only a lifelong friend about this, my old mountain-climbing partner, Leeds Davis. He offered it back to me as proof of reincarnation, which I'd been skeptical about. What I saw was the actual past, he said. I was still unsure about that.

Flash forward: Nearly ten years later, when I had met and married Meredith, she told me she'd recently had several dreams that we were artists who roomed together in Greenwich Village in the 1920s. We were both gay men, but I was ashamed of that, would not let anyone else know, and was generally difficult about it.

Her dreams astounded me. But now I couldn't escape opening the door to reincarnation as a genuine possibility. Meredith had always believed in it firmly. In fact, we've made an agreement about meeting in our next lives. In this life we didn't meet until I was fifty-eight, and we want more time together than is likely on this go-round. She is the melody in my hymn to life. Since I understand that we are both energy, and energy can neither be created or destroyed, I know that we can walk the world in more than one incarnation.

That was the gift of my first Naraya dance.

17. OVERWHELMED

The next year I went back to the dance, but the locale had changed to a YMCA camp a short way upstate in New York. Everything else was the same, even my accommodations in Manhattan. In fact, Juliette was becoming one of my best friends.

I had changed my preparations a little. I wore an eagle foot, with all the claws, around my neck. This alarmed several of the other dancers, who warned me that if Spirit knocked me down, the claws might cut me. But I loved this totem and felt sure that it would never hurt me.

When we were singing the Lakota eagle song, I sang super-enthusiastically. I loved this tribute to the messenger of the great powers, because an eagle had brought me a supreme gift when I needed it, the last pages of *Stone Song*. I tilted my head back and opened my mouth wide to call fiercely to the skies.

An eagle dived down my throat and ate my heart.

I fell like a redwood toppling from a great height. My eagle claw didn't bother me at all, but in the world beyond I was attacked violently.

This is the extraordinary, amazing feeling of a vision: As usual, I was fully aware of what was going on around me in the ordinary world, which was a secondary compartment of my consciousness. At the same time I was in the seeing-beyond state, and there I was enduring an ultra-vivid and ultra-painful experience. I was lying naked on a stone projection on a rocky ridge on a high mountain, which I somehow knew was in Tibet. Vultures were stripping the skin off my body.

Though I knew I was dead, I felt terrible pain. When the vultures finished with my skin, they began tearing my organs out.

Back in the compartment of ordinary consciousness, I remembered books like Mircea Eliade's *Shamanism* and recognized what was happening to me as a Tibetan sky burial, or what is called an excarnation. Early Siberian shamans commonly experienced visions of themselves being stripped in this way, and as I recalled, it was often interpreted as the death of the old self to make a place for the new self, so the shaman could see what others could not.

When I got beyond the pain, I thought, chuckling, 'Win, if you're going to have a vision, why must you pick such a cliché?' Yet I knew this seeing was a way to new understanding.

Meanwhile, in the mundane reality, Juliette was bending over me or kneeling by me. She called one of the other helpers over, a man I didn't know. She said, "He's going very deep. Will you stay right with him?"

And so I got a helper. I was aware of him sitting next to me, and felt comforted by that.

Somehow the trance state took command. I had abruptly gone somewhere very strange. Now I was on my hands and knees on the ground. Some possum-like animal was leading me down into a hole, and it gave me strict instructions to hold tight to its tail and let it take me where it wanted to go.

I don't like caves and hate tunnels, especially those barely wide enough for my shoulders. The confinement, the dust up the nose and in the eyes, the inability to turn back, the fear and loathing of going forward—all afflicted me.

In time we came to a rocky chamber. The possum, or whatever it was, disappeared. Somehow I had arrived at my destination.

The chamber was about four feet wide and high and six feet long, so there wasn't a lot of room for me. At the far end was the black coil that is commonly seen on the backs of refrigerators.

Then I saw that it wasn't a refrigerator coil at all. It was a big rattlesnake, curved in a way a snake would never coil, the tail part on the bottom, a stack of loops rising vertically, and the head on top.

I am deathly afraid of snakes.

It struck at my face.

Again and again—hiss-hiss, fangs flashing in my face.

Then I realized it wasn't striking. It was toying with me, hissing and faking strikes from all angles, torturing me, and perhaps getting me paralyzed with fear before striking the fatal blow.

Suddenly, an idea and a truckload of courage flooded into me all at once. I knew exactly what I needed to do. I reached out and grabbed the snake by both ends. *And tied it into a Celtic love knot.* I looked at my work with satisfaction and put it back.

A Celtic Love Knot

I gazed at it with immense happiness. I had transformed evil into love. Miracle of miracles.

I drifted back all the way into a normal state of consciousness. Apparently Spirit had had its say.

I listened. The memory of the Celtic love knot warmed me— evil into love. I thought of other meanings in what I had seen. The most elusive was being killed by the vultures so that a new self could re-animate me.

I decided I could do nothing about that except live my life and stay open to change.

18. $\mathscr{W}$ALKING
THE WALK

I have had other visionary experiences in the years since those described in these pages. I often feel like I am in a state of continual renewal since I shed the old Win and began to walk forward as a New Man. I have spent my days not walking according to some set of rules but to living by my insights in the present moment, seeing with the single eye of my heart, remembering always that we are all related, treating everyone I meet with human kindness—being as good a human being as I can.

I have set down for the reader the big revolutions of my life, starting out as a Southern Baptist, becoming a Great White Doubter, finding myself bewildered by the seas of life, and finally opening myself more fully, beginning to learn, to see, to understand in a generous spirit, and so on.

Now I will foreshorten the rest of the story, remembering my great experiences and treasuring the clarity and beauty within them.

After having my old self excarnated by vultures and a new self invited in, a self of greater love of life and the life force, I was still a man at loose ends, newly divorced, and broke. Since I had completed *Stone Song*, I was even disoriented as a writer. I had no ideas what path to take next.

Since this is a spiritual memoir, I will speak of my journey of the spirit since that time.

I moved from the south side of Yellowstone Park to the north side, looking for love. I didn't find it. However, for a year and a half I was privileged to go into the sweat lodge every weekend with a group of Crow and Blackfeet men. For the second year, as the oldest man in the lodge, I was asked to lead the sweat—to pour water on the hot rocks, say traditional prayers, and invite other men to pray and to lay down the troubles of everyday life.

A sweat lodge, a low hut of willow branches covered with blankets, with red-hot rocks in the middle. When water is poured on the rocks, the lodge fills with steam. Here one figure holds an eagle wing, used before the ceremony to spread smoke around the lodge for cleansing, and the other holds a gourd rattle. The spirit of a bird, perhaps an eagle, hovers over the lodge. Painting by Richard Packo, photo courtesy of the Naraya Cultural Preservation Council.

In the last month of my time in Montana I was invited to participate in a Crow vision quest high in the Big Horn Mountains. It became the only five-day quest I've ever done, all five days without food or water, though the deprivation didn't bother me. At the end I got the blessing of having my chest pierced, being tied to the sacred tree, and breaking free. Paradoxically, I was not given the blessing of a vision on that occasion, the only time I have sought and not seen beyond.

19. AWARENESS

I had gone to Montana in hope of finding love with a woman I knew. Now, at the end of a year and a half there, I knew that quest was futile. I decided to return to Jackson and be near my two sons. Meanwhile, I was set to do a book tour.

On the tour I had lunch with a woman, Marcia Meredith, I had met at the Jackson Hole Writers Conference the previous summer. I had felt a strong vibration of attraction to her then. Now that magnetism seemed really powerful. Over the next few months we emailed each other often. However, I told myself to walk my path consciously, keeping the clarity I had, not getting ahead of myself. I reminded myself continually that I wanted to stay in Jackson near my sons for a while and revitalize my life as a writer.

When Meredith came to Jackson for the writers conference that summer, I discovered powerfully that I had found the love of my life. Everything we did for the next few months confirmed that feeling of certainty, and we made a lifetime commitment to each other. As I write, we have been together for more than twenty years, and look forward to being together for many more years and lifetimes.

We both wanted to live in the Southwest, and so moved near Monument Valley. It has some of the world's most spectacular scenery, an in-my-face-every-day reminder of what a supreme artist Mother Earth is. We human artists vibrate strongly to the earth's vast creativity.

From that time forward to today I have kept up my Lakota spiritual practice, but living far from my Shoshone, Lakota, and Crow friends, I've been obliged to do it on my own.

In addition to our family wedding ceremony, Meredith and I had a legal ceremony and a Navajo ceremony, which included a blessing upon our new house. We tell each other every day that getting to love another human being so fully is a gift beyond all others. We treasure each other now and forever.

For ten years I had a sweat lodge on the property Meredith and I owned and used it to pour a sweat when I had willing companions. Eventually, though, I complied with Meredith's request that I no longer sweat—she said I came out looking like a lobster. (Sometimes my sweat companions did mention that I poured very hot sweats.)

So now on my own: I still pray daily so that I have time to express my gratitude to all the Powers. I meditate. I smoke my pipe, offering the smoke to the four directions, Father Sky, and Mother Earth. I find more and more to be grateful for—the manifestation power of the life force on this planet, what the Lakota people call *taku skan skan*.

I stand in wonder at the energy that runs the universe and salute it as the Great Mystery—*taku skan skan* for sure. Along with M. Scott Peck, I say *Miracle, miracle, all is miracle*.

More spiritual practice on my own: Recently I have added Transcendental Meditation to my days. Though I am still an infant meditator, I am committed to it. Spirit comes to us in many ways.

Maintaining my Lakota practice: Beyond remembering to see with the single eye of the heart, I still seek sometimes to see beyond, beating my drum hypnotically, inviting Spirit to enter and give me wisdom. I am able to get important gifts in that way. However, because of age and my unwillingness to be apart from Meredith, I no longer do the vision quests of multiple days. (Also, my physician has ruled out fasting and thirsting, even for a single day.) Nor do I miss the longer quests. Recently a single day of devoted seeking brought me a surprising and marevllous insight.

However, Clyde is considering offering his new form of the Naraya Dance, the Dance for All Peoples, online. If those ceremonies take place, I will sing and dance enthusiastically.

Pueblo Bonito, my favorite of the pueblos in Chaco Canyon

Last objects of devotion: The desert and mountain Southwest, where we live, is full of sacred sites. That term might include sites of natural landscape, like Monument Valley and Rainbow Bridge, but I am thinking mostly of sites built for worship of the Powers— places constructed hundreds of years ago by the Anasazi people for worship. My personal favorite of these sites is Chaco Canyon National Monument, a concentration of fifteen sets of pueblos built in the tenth through the twelfth centuries, wonderfully well preserved, and most of them within a short walk from modern parking lots. These buildings were family homes that surround great kivas, round chambers deep as wells, centers for prayer. They were also used to observe and mark the movements of the sun and moon.

Anasazi people lived within a huge circle, more than a hundred miles around, traveled regularly to these Chaco Canyon kivas for worship. This was the center of their spiritual lives.

For visitors these places still palpitate with a sense of the sacred. It enters with every breath.

Visits to these places, like visits to the Vatican, strike us with an awareness of the omnipresence of Spirit.

Some places on earth have a heartbeat of the sacred that is palpable. Perhaps, if we are aware, all places do.

Brothers, sisters, love this earth, the air you breathe, the water you drink, the sun on your skin. Love life, love your life.

Every breath is a miracle. Celebrate it.

20. LAST THOUGHTS

What I've told you here is simply my own experience. It's literally true, all of it. This has been the path I've walked, and I'm about to tell you where I now find myself along the road.

In some ways visions are like hearing new melodies in my head. I don't know where they come from, but I welcome them and enjoy them.

So here's a question: Do I now believe in god (God, if you prefer), the fellow I cast off on the October day in 1957, when I was at the Bible school? Am I religious now?

In a friend's garden in Nepal, after weeks of trekking in the Himalayas, I had an amazing realization: God is love, because this entire planet is a spectacular act of love for those of us privileged to spend our days here. I swam in gratitude then and there. Did I return to my first religion?

No, in my long search I haven't seen any sign of a guy with a long, white beard and dressed in a robe who hands out mandates like the Ten Commandments and at some point chooses to consign each of us to heaven or hell forever. That doesn't mean I see no value in his sayings, or the sayings of his representatives. But I haven't found him anywhere, and I don't think he's at the center of the universe. I have been in communication with Mother Earth, Father Sky, and the winds of the four directions, and am grateful for the blessings they give us. For me they are the center.

Again, am I religious?

When I asked Joe Marshall "What is the essence of Lakota religion?," he answered with words that now speak for me. "We Lakota don't have a religion.

We see reality, see the way things really are. You white people don't see it because you've trained yourselves not to."

I ride with Joe. I see my own life now as centered on the spiritual.

After years of seeking, I recognize that there is a single force in the world—what moves everything that moves, animates everything, makes it what it is—people the unique beings they are, the birds birds, the cats cats, the stars stars, and so on. *Taku skan skan*—I revere the Life Force, that unimaginably prodigious, unimaginably fecund, unimaginably creative energy.

On this planet life is in love with life. The earth is singing a song composed in the key of love.

And I want to sing out my great love for this earth and this life. Walt Whitman sounded his barbaric yawp over the rooftops of the world. Here's mine:

GLORY HALLELUJAH, WHAT A WORLD!

Whoops! Self-correction to let my spirit animal speak—

GLORY HO-O-OWLELUJAH, WHAT A WORLD!

I also think often of how I am simply a latter-day cell of one great organism, one of great spirit, humankind. I am grateful to the billions of grandfathers and grandmothers who came before me, for at least two hundred and fifty million years of *homo sapiens,* and I say to them, every single one, *Mitaku oyasin*—We are all related. And we have many, many more grandfathers and grandmothers than the single species *homo sapiens*—the four-legged creatures, the winged, the finny ones, the crawlers, the rooted, and more and more and more, a conception that ultimately includes Mother Earth herself and all her progeny. All, all, we are all grandfathers and grandmothers, bearers of the one sacred fire, the divine spark, the gleam that is everything called life.

I cannot say these two words with enough vigor, or enough reverence, or enough joy—*Mitaku oyasin*. We are all related.

And all are embraced, at least in the moments of my outreaching consciousness—in the bond of my love.

This, truly, is eternal life.

Mitaku oyasin.

Behind us, so many grasses, so many snows.

Before us, so many grasses, so many snows.

Father Sky, thank you. Mother Earth, thank you.
I give you my greatest gratitude,
My deepest love,

Win Blevins

Printed in Great Britain
by Amazon

56098072R00061

Fishing for Dr Richard

BOB KIMMERLING